SECRETS OF
THE DIVINE BUSINESS CODE

"Mentoring you in a sacred space, we empower and enable each other. Creating your Divine Feminine Business Masterpiece."

KELLY VIKINGS

KELLY VIKINGS

THE DIVINE BUSINESS LEADER

Intuition
CONNECTION
Alignment
TRUTH
Strength

KELLY VIKINGS

MY VISION

'To empower women in business, to step into their Divine Feminine Ultimate Power'

MY MISSION

'To ensure every woman, from all corners of the world, steps into her heart space, discovers her truth, connects to her Divine Ultimate Power, to evoke blissful **Divine Alignment™**.
Building strong business foundations discovered in the secrets of **The Divine Business Code™** creating Divine Strength, Success and Wealth'

Disclaimer

Although the author has made every effort to ensure that the information in this book was correct at press time, the author does not assume and hereby disclaim any liability to any party for any loss, damage, or disruption caused by errors or omissions, whether such errors or omissions result from negligence, accident, or any other cause.

I have tried to recreate events, locales and conversations from my memories of them. In order to maintain their anonymity in some instances I have changed the names of individuals and places, I may have changed some identifying characteristics and details such as physical properties, occupations and places of residence.

Copyright © 2021 by Kelly Vikings
ISBN 13:978-1-913728-35-9
All rights reserved.
No part of this book may be reproduced in any form or by any electronic or mechanical means, including information storage and retrieval systems, without written permission from the author, except for the use of brief quotations in a book review.

authors
AND CO.

CONTENTS

Preface	xi
Welcome	xxv

1. Introducing Secrets of The Divine Business Code — 1
2. Let's Talk Entrepreneur Truths! — 12
3. Your Unique Divine Business Code TM — 22
4. Creating your Vision, Your Purpose, Your Why — 33
5. Defining your Ultimate Mission — 43
6. Divine Business Blueprint — 50
7. The True Essence of You — 68
8. Super Connectivity — 78
9. Your Brand — 89
10. Your Superpowers — 102
11. Powerful Organic Marketing — 110
12. The Power of you! — 124
13. Divinely Guided Sales — 138
14. Global Connectivity, Building a Global Online Business. — 150
15. Miracle Foundations — 158
16. The Power of Conversion — 177
17. Launching with Impact — 188
18. The Power of Pause — 202
19. Resilience and Growth — 210
20. Creating your Legacy — 218

DEDICATION

*This book is dedicated to you!
To all the fiercely driven women business warriors out there, daring to elevate their lives and create a brighter future for themselves.
We RISE together and by stepping into your Divine Feminine energies you are leading the way for other women, future generations to navigate a more connected, united, aligned and inclusive future, consciously creating change in a world that's shifting.
Bravely and courageously its time, right now to discover your divine ultimate power, to evoke and awaken your souls' divine blueprint to manifest and create a future that aligns with the essence of all you are becoming, no fear, limitless, quantum leaping beyond your wildest imagination and dreams.*

PREFACE

Chapter Contents.

I encourage you to use this book to help support your business growth.

To make this easier for you I have outlined each chapter, referenced what powerful subjects are covered, for you to use as handy reference points to refer to in the future.

Welcome

What to expect as this is NOT your usual, standard, business book!

PREFACE

1. Introducing Secrets of The Divine Business Code

- How this book will support you to start, grow and scale your business.

2. Let's Talk Entrepreneur Truths!

- Questions to start your entrepreneurial journey
- Risks and what it's really like to be an entrepreneur
- What others will say, how to dig deep
- Why you are taking this big leap of faith in yourself

3. Your Unique Divine Business Code

- Creating your unique business blueprint
- Understanding the Divine Business Code
- Discovering your Divine Ultimate Power
- Your Divine Destiny and Ultimate Life Path
- Discovering your unique Divine Alignment & why this is so important to decoding your business success
- Divine Feminine and how to create a business the aligned way!

4. Creating your Vision, Your Purpose, Your Why

- Your Why!
- Discovering your fierce driving force
- Having clarity of vision
- Creating a powerful vision statement

5. Defining your Ultimate Mission

- Why having a mission statement is so powerful
- Why a mission statement underpins your business decisions
- Creating your Masterplan & Mission statement

6. Divine Business Blueprint

- Your Business Plan - Why everyone needs a Divine Business Blueprint
- Business strategy, modelling and smarter systems that support your business unique Divine Business Blueprint
- Building blocks to creating your quantum business strength, success & wealth

- Numeric energy and guest writer Jo Soley on how knowing your numbers increases your numbers in business.

7. The True Essence of You

- Investing in yourself and connecting to the REAL version of who you are
- YOU are the heartbeat, the foundation of your business, its most valuable asset
- Money & Mindset tips
- Miracle Foundations - Commitment, Consistency, Discipline and Energy

8. Super Connectivity

- Connection is THE most important superpower
- Getting results and HOW to create a connected, engaged and responsive following
- Growing your Audience, through powerful social media marketing
- Numbers mean NOTHING if you don't connect to them
- Taking your audience on a journey
- What stands in your way, or is stopping you from

being seen on social media, and how to turn fear or negative thoughts into powerful drivers
- Your clients are the heartbeat of your business - CONNECTION is everything explained!

9. Your Brand

- Creating your own brand identity
- What does your brand stand for, what does it promise to deliver
- Speaking from the heart and removing the B.S
- Creating a Powerful Bio, who you are, what your do, how you achieve it, who you work for, and what is the impact of your work!
- What is a brand, what does it mean, how does it show up?
- Powerful Brand Values, how to create your TOP 5.
- Powerful Brand Promises, how to create your TOP 5.

10. Your Superpowers

- Divine Alignment - in complete flow, magnetic, ultra-powerful and attractive
- Confidence is your BELIEF

- Superpowers are your unique identity, your niche, your business positioning
- Using your superpowers to scale and grow your business for ultimate impact and limitless results

11. Powerful Organic Marketing

- How to create authentic, emotive, connected, and divinely aligned powerful organic marketing strategies
- Key marketing words that resonate on every level
- Powerful Social Media framework that excites you and your clients
- Powerful STORY framework to share your unique story giving tips on how to create maximum impact and overcome limiting beliefs, sharing your STORY confidently
- How to connect even more deeply by founding your own online communities

12. The Power of you!

- The Power of you! Letting go of all that stops you
- Prosperity mindset and having an abundance of all your heart desires

PREFACE

- Self love, compassion and honouring yourself before anyone or anything else
- Manifesting your own divine destiny, the power of your thoughts, beliefs and words
- Trusting in the process and being divinely guided every step of the way
- 5 Powerful C's - Connection, Communication, Community, Collaboration, Contribution. How they support you to grow an aligned business that serves your soul

13. Divinely Guided Sales

- WE all need to sell something! Let's do it the divine way
- What to avoid and how to not make mistakes that will cost you time, money and effort
- Creating your own sales process that creates a unique, customer journey and experience
- Sales underpinned by integrity and compassion and guest writer Lisa Johnson sharing her Top Tips on how to align your sales process, to ensure you always come from a place of compassion and truth.

14. Global Connectivity, Building a Global Online Business

- The core differences of Offline V's Online Businesses
- Scaling your teams to fuel expansion and growth in your business
- Global limitless connectivity - What this means
- One to One V's One to Many and how this can work for your clients or NOT

15. Miracle Foundations

- Why every business requires solid foundations and how to build yours
- Smarter business strategies, the importance of Refining and Reviewing
- Your Business Model - I share the ascension business model that creates a powerful client journey that aligns beautifully, part of my Divine Alignment programme
- Powerful online business growth strategies
- Social media strategies, including gifting you a weekly 'social media grid' to help you design your weekly/30 day content

- Building and growing FB and online Communities
- PR, Media and Creating limitless opportunities
- Website and how/when to create yours
- Email list growth and connection strategies
- Tech strategies building smart systems and processes in your business to support your business growth
- Cash Flow and Talent the importance of building solid foundations

16. The Power of Conversion

- How to consistently convert your audience to paid clients
- Powerful and supportive mindset strategies
- Onboarding of new clients - Let's talk processes and client journey
- Excelling and raising your standards for the best client care
- What are lead magnets and how to be creative and create them
- Podcast and TV shows creating even more opportunities for conversion
- Tips to create lead magnets, trip wires and LANDING pages that powerfully convert

- Asking for the sale... What is often a simple underestimated secret weapon!
- How to turn setbacks and rejection into steppingstones to success

17. Launching with Impact

- The importance of having a plan and proven launch method
- How to save your time and get launched
- Your launch style and what it means to you
- How to create your own launch strategy incl timescale, target audience, powerful step by step marketing strategies
- What doesn't work and will cost you time, money and results!
- What to do post launching and why this supports each subsequent launch

18. The Power of Pause

- Surrendering to the Power of Pause and WHY as women business leaders and rising warriors it's so important to protect your energy, practise gratitude, and honour ourselves, avoiding overwhelm and burnout.

- Embodying the power of the Divine Feminine and how this can evoke balance and harmony in your business creating even more success.

19. Resilience and Growth

- In a NEW world where everything is changing so fast, and our bodies are awakening to a new way forwards in business the ability to become resilient and have a healthy perspective is so powerful
- Aligning inner and outer worlds to create total divine alignment
- The importance of a business plan and how to be diligent in working with it to support growth in scaling up your business
- Identifying blind spots in your business, protecting your empire
- Markers for business growth
- Knowing your talent, numbers, cash flow in business

20. Creating your Legacy

- 19 TOP TIPS to create your legacy and overcome anything that comes your way!

PREFACE

- Important and powerful messages guided from me to my readers.
- Self-Love - It will always start with you.
- The past is not the measure of your future.
- Free and limitless
- Not the equation of anyone else
- Build life on your terms - An exceptional life does not just happen.
- Get out of your head into your heart space
- Learn to honour your energy and fill your cup first
- Be clear on your WHY
- Be prepared to face setbacks - Success will TEST YOU
- Be clear on your MISSION - have a North Star and be focused inside your lane
- Changing LIVES starts with One Person, One Vision, One Action
- Make a contribution
- Embody leading with LOVE
- Creating your Legacy
- Celebrate your wins
- Remember nothing can hold you back; you are free
- You are destined for even greater success
- You are limitless

PREFACE

Resources are available to all readers. Please visit www.kellyvikings.com

Download and print your free workbook, to complete all guided tasks inside book.

WELCOME

For those of you who don't yet know me, I'm Kelly Vikings, your business mentor for the duration of this book and beyond. Always leading with love, I'm highly intuitive, a little bit Kick Ass and everything in between!

Thank you for taking the time to read Secrets of The Divine Business Code. I truly believe there are no coincidences: you are ready to discover the secrets to unlocking your own unique Divine Business Code. This book is a catalyst to decoding your conscious business success. Let's consciously commit to enjoying working together.

I'm much more than a business mentor, I am...

WELCOME

The Divine Business Leader

Empowering women to shine in their own light, stepping into their true power, with strength, truth and Viking Warrior wings.

It's time to live boldly with your inner belief and confidence, share your TRUTHS and be proud of everything you are.

Together we are limitless!

It's my mission to ensure every woman, from all corners of the world, steps into her heart space, discovers her truth, and connects to her Divine Ultimate Power, to evoke blissful Divine Alignment... building strong business foundations to create Divine Success and Wealth, and always being nurtured in an impactful way.

Your 'Step by Step' Book experience

I didn't want to write a book that was just average!

I wanted to create an experience, a book that would be your Divine Business Manual.

WELCOME

It's like I'm with you, mentoring you every step of the way.

I encourage you to connect with me, reach out to me and feed back to me your own experiences at any stage.

Here are a few ways you may experience this book:

- Read and place me gently on the bookcase
- Read me and head over to the links and download the free resources
- Read and connect with myself and the other mentors I've included within the blueprint of your book. Your book is absolutely about 'connection' and expanding your knowledge and networks
- Read me and complete the workbook style activities; take them away and implement them into your business
- Remember to take notes throughout; use them for your business growth and as continued resources

Don't be afraid to scribble in your book or use a highlighter. This is your Divine Business Manual for you to use in the way that feels aligned to you. Here are some tips...

- Keep notes of your ideas
- Note how you feel whilst reading the chapters

- Take the chapters' key 'takeaways' and write them in your own words
- Make notes of anything that inspires you to take action
- List key focus points to continue to work more deeply on later
- Make a note of reference points in the book
- Make a note of any NEW desires you consciously set
- List who you wish to connect with and why

Each chapter has so many invaluable KEY trainings. Each chapter is briefly summarised in the contents. If you're working on an aspect in your business you can open to any part of this book in the future to support you, not just today, but at any point in the future as you continue to grow and scale your business.

INTRODUCING SECRETS OF THE DIVINE BUSINESS CODE

No more hiding in the shadows… it's your time to shine!

In today's NEW world, there are constantly challenging pressures that business leaders face.

However, whilst dealing with these challenges, so many people avoid working on the most valuable asset in their business… themselves!

This is why this book comes from a place of knowing. I've experienced all of this myself and now I gift you successful strategies that work, delivering ways to effectively improve both you and your business. Ultimately these are your inner and outer worlds, creating Divine Alignment!

It saddens me to see many business leaders overwhelmed or afraid to stand in their truths, held back by their lack of clarity of vision, purpose and business strategy, or confidence and self-belief. Taking time for you and embracing 'The Power of Pause' creates space for you to work on these areas. You'll then be able to seek and attract an abundance of growth and resilience in your business. We dig deeper into this later on.

When you come from a place of truth, abundance and belief, it's far easier to take time for self-love, to gain clarity of your vision and to be consistently disciplined in your business. You can show up as the REAL essence of who you are and who you are destined to become!

I've witnessed so many business leaders facing or overcoming setbacks in life. These experiences chip away at them, hold them back and allow self-doubt and procrastination to creep in, with too much pressure or expectations being placed upon them by themselves or external contributors. This leads to many incredible business leaders resisting the opportunity to shine in their own unique light, which seriously affects their confidence, productivity and performance.

As we step through a New Millennium, we're seeing a shift in energies around the globe as the balance between feminine and masculine energies are being aligned and restored. We've lived through an imbalance for so long. Business leaders are tapping into their emotions, intuition, feeling guided to share their truths and vulnerabilities, and a strong desire to honour themselves and protect their energies. This shift of energy is creating waves, as we learn to embody the Divine Feminine as women and men unite.

We are here to become our truest and highest expression. Real growth is the Divine Feminine way.

We have limitless, global connectivity and opportunities like never before. Our world is changing the way we work. A new world is born. This for me is so exciting - organic growth, limitless connectivity, a true sense of working in unity. It's incredible to see so many business leaders resisting the B.S. and seeking out truths, integrity and transparency.

There are so many business leaders consciously building purpose driven businesses: heart led, strong, integrity driven legacies. Unity, equality, inclusion and of course connection, contribution and community have never been more important when defining and rebuilding our lives, businesses, economies, societies and our world, for our future generations.

It was never a burning desire or lifelong dream to write a book. Sometimes I believe we are called to deliver our value to the world, innately knowing it has the power to make a real difference to empower and transform lives. In this case, lives and businesses!

Have you ever woken up in the middle of the night and received a significant download from source, that led you to having a strong desire and urgency to do something, often something that stretches you, and is from a place of service to others?

This is exactly how this book was created. I woke up and knew I had to write this for you, its title etched before me, the book blueprint divinely gifted to me. Hence it's here today for you. My work is always guided. I'm honoured to share it with you. My desire is that it makes a significant contribution to elevating your life and business.

February 26th 2019, a day I will never forget!

This was the very day, after eight months of drawn-out exhaustion, stress, overwhelm, and holding on to so much guilt and shame, that the doors to my previous business closed, after twelve years. I saw my dreams, everything I'd poured my life into, disappear in an instant. Those eight months of juggling and hiding in fear, crippled by immense shame, were the hardest months of my entire life.

The aftershock saw my name plastered in the press, bad publicity that only deepened and exposed the full extent of what had happened. I wasn't the only person in this story. There was not just one reason my business had failed – there were many.

Taking these invaluable business lessons, I learnt they could help others. Standing tall in my truths, talking and sharing them, helped other business leaders to avoid the same mistakes. It helped to open their eyes to their blind spots, often missed in scaling and growing a business enterprise. If you don't know, you don't know, so I share what I do know to really help others.

In the following eighteen months, I saw everything I'd worked so hard for disappear. Financial wealth, material possessions and the security of our family home, all taken during my bankruptcy. I had lost everything…

I was terribly unwell: the weight of all of this saw me hide deep in my emotions, and I sank into depression. I was suicidal and completely broken. It took the hardest of days, knowing how I could end this and silently questioning how I could sneak away to step out of this life, to knowing that I could not carry on like this.

The only thing that brought me back from this deep state of numbness and anxiousness and being completely broken, was my partner and our children. I had two options, to check out for good or to STAND UP and share my truths and start from ZERO! As I'm writing this for you, I guess you know which option I chose.

I decided to trust in myself and yet I continued to struggle. I had no idea who I was anymore. I felt a desperate sense of wanting to rediscover myself.

I recall the day. It was a sunny one in September 2019 and my partner and I had taken ourselves off to the woods camping. I urgently wanted to know what I was going to become, desperate to know what my life may look like. Martin, my life and business partner, who's a coach, suggested to calm down and take a day or two to just relax! To breathe! To enjoy being in nature.

Out of nowhere, he began asking me questions that led me to see what my new life purpose was. In that moment I knew that EVERYTHING I'd experienced and courageously overcome was no coincidence. It was all part of a far greater divine purpose the universe had prepared me for.

I rediscovered who I was, created a NEW vision. I knew I wanted it to come from a place of LOVE and wanting to genuinely give back to others.

I had no idea what I was unlocking or how powerful this would be, not just for me, but also for people like you too! I knew that there were many business skills, practical experiences, that I had learnt over 23 years, that could be passed on to other business leaders. I just didn't realise how powerful that would be.

Everything happens for a reason; your life destiny is mapped out before you. The more you resist or fail to see the signs or understand the lessons served, the more the universe will present you with them, sometimes forcing you to stop or circumstances forcing you to take notice!

I believe we all need to trust that inner knowing, our calling, and discover the true essence of ourselves to unlock our true path, to discover our Divine Alignment, unleashing our truest, highest self.

I've written this book to show you what is possible. To share everything I know to be true, to really support you in every aspect of being a business leader. I've ridden my own personal journey, taking extreme setbacks, limited resources, lack of cash flow, lack of support and created my own comeback, against all the odds... you can too!

We are all LIMITLESS. We are not defined by our past!

Most things in life are possible! It starts by making the decision to take action, and to create your own foundations in business, a Divine Business Blueprint. This rewards you with crystal clear clarity, discipline and focus, avoiding comparisonitis and building smarter strategies, systems and processes that support you and your business growth. You will learn how to grow an organic audience and connect on a deeper level, breeding loyalty and a far more meaningful business than ever before.

I believe I can truly help you to become a better leader. We've all bought books we haven't read to the end, courses we haven't completed, masterclasses we didn't show up to. I get it, life gets in the way...

I'm gifting you some of the most precious, divinely guided knowledge and experiences that have the Power to elevate both you and your business to an entirely NEW level. You'll feel in complete flow, it will come with ease, it will work with you, not against you, and you will see results that you never realised were ever possible!

I'm joining you for the journey, every step of the way. We'll make it possible. Rather than chucking this book on the side with the rest, actually read it and ask yourself questions, then take aligned, inspired and grounded action. Use the strategies and approach that I share... they work.

I know I can help you. I come to you with many years of leadership and business growth experience. I'm absolutely not just talking the talk. I've lived it, experienced it on every level and walked it! After what I've been through, I want to make a difference to you. I know I can. Trust me; I'll help you to achieve the extraordinary.

My promise to you is that I will not share anything I haven't tried, tested or delivered myself. Nor will I give you any bullshit. Everything I share comes from a place of truth and is delivered with love and integrity. I know how important this is: you want to know REAL entrepreneurial truths, not just the shiny! You'll read all about what works and what doesn't.

My promise is for you to feel as though I'm personally guiding you, mentoring you, using some great tools to work with through the chapters, that I know will give you what you need to gain clarity, direction, confidence and belief in your work. I even introduce you to some of my mentors, people who've inspired me, who have helped me transform my life.

I promise this is much more than a book. This is an experience that will set you on the path to self-discovery, driving your business with clarity and purpose, giving you all the knowledge and tools you need to realise real organic growth and deliver the results you desire, and leading you to fulfil your divine destiny and achieve all your wildest of dreams. Many questions you have left unanswered will be answered. I also want you to connect with me and ask me anything. Remember I am with you every step of the way.

Many people may question the amount I am giving away so freely in this book. However, I come from a place of wanting to exchange real value and give tangible business advice that drives and delivers real results.

This book is divinely guided, which could be viewed as a bit 'fluffy' or 'woo woo', but I can guarantee you that if you read and implement the vital lessons, the knowledge I share with you, you absolutely will see a HUGE shift in mindset, approach to your business, the ease with which you attract business and the way you WIN loyal clients. This will lead to an abundance of business that will reward you financially, but it's so much more than that.

This GIVE without expectations approach is something I do a lot in my own business, aligning with my own true values. I want you to take this freely and climb to that next level. You will achieve so much more. Working with me directly will increase the results you have even more. I trust in the process that if you feel I am the right person to help you achieve that you will connect with me and make that happen.

You will LOVE this book and you will absolutely LOVE the results you gain in both your life and business - I promise you that! I hope you enjoy reading it as much as I have enjoyed writing it for you.

Are you ready? Let's do this!

LET'S TALK ENTREPRENEUR TRUTHS!

Time to talk straight and for me to deliver some truths before we go any further.

I want to ask you a few questions.

Are you aspiring to be an entrepreneur?

Do you believe you have what it takes to be a successful business owner?

How did your entrepreneurial journey begin?

I know each and every one of you reading this has a unique reason WHY.

Did you feel prepared for taking that initial brave step, that huge leap?

I would hazard a guess, for most of us, we weren't prepared.

Did you realise what it would take to create your own successful business?

We're often marred by what we see others achieve and don't always consider what it took to get them to that point.

If you're at the very beginning of your entrepreneurial journey, does it excite you, scare you or both?

You may hear that being an entrepreneur is like riding a roller coaster - many ups and downs. This is true and why you may feel excited and scared at the same time.

Have you been a business owner and know only too well the extreme highs and lows that running a business can present to you?

I've interviewed hundreds of entrepreneurs and none of them has had an easy path, yet when we run our own business, for many there is absolutely no way of going back to a

9-5 job. It's a real energy, an entrepreneurial spirit that drives us!

Are you reading this book with a knowing of how tough being a business owner has been, yet how finally it become worth it? You're living your dream!

Take a look at what you've achieved, see how you inspire others: feels good doesn't it? It is absolutely possible. I'm glad you've joined me for this new business journey.

You see, we're all at completely different stages of our entrepreneurial journey. When you're new to becoming the leader of your own destiny, embracing the solopreneur badge of honour, it's easy to feel overwhelmed with fear or what ifs!

The entrepreneurial journey is not for everyone. There's a growing percentage of the population of this planet who dream of setting up their own business. Even more so in the younger generation, who may be dreaming of self employment and avoiding the traditional 'perceived safety zone' of employment. They tend to be purpose driven, they move towards ethical enterprises, they love sustainability, they want flexible and financially rewarding lives, and they aspire to have their own businesses.

Whether it's because you don't like your current job - it quite frankly bores the pants off you - or you feel there's more and you're worth more, now you think it's the right time to step into your own power, to be your own boss. You believe you'll earn more money starting a business on your own and it'll give you flexibility. Maybe that's the flexibility to work around your lifestyle or home commitments. There could be many reasons. I know if you're stepping away from what you see as security it will be terrifying, but the more you wait the longer you will live with regrets.

With all this in mind, I want you to hear some TRUTHS and really share invaluable feedback before you enter the entrepreneurial zone.

Before I do, I want you to really know that you are ready. I see so many entrepreneurs not having a plan, not believing in themselves or starting without any, or very limited resources. It's ok, it's all part of your experience of stepping into this new world. This book will give you some incredible short cuts. I wish I had known these when I first started my own business. I'm certain many will agree they wish they had too!

There's a significantly high percentage of small businesses that fail in their first five years, over 50% of small businesses. Yet the figures don't tell the real story or truths and I wouldn't let this discourage you in pursuing your new venture. If anything, I want it to echo the importance of building really strong foundations, framework and systems. All of this I help you to be aware of as you read the rest of this book. Be prepared to initially work smarter and harder, for longer term business success.

You're taking the biggest leap of faith in yourself you'll ever take. It may be far better than you ever anticipated. It may be the most phenomenal experience of your life, take you to places you never dreamt of. It may be the most incredible HIGH. You may even have success for many years and then lose everything. You may not ever realise your highest vision.

I can guarantee you, if you're new to stepping into this world, it will NOT be plain sailing all the time and you must be prepared to overcome challenges and make risky decisions. Some will pay off and others won't... you will never stop learning new things, that's for sure!

You may believe being an entrepreneur is easy, that it will all magically come your way, and luck will be on your side. I'm here to say it rarely does, and in business there's no such thing as luck. You create your own opportunities, and you design your own business rewards, based on the action you take on a daily basis. Success will absolutely test you.

I know when I set up my business I had very few resources and it could have stopped me. Not having the financial collateral will put many ambitious entrepreneurs off, delay them from taking that the next step. Financial security is a BIG anchor to staying in your 9-5 and often an equally weighted anchor to keeping you in your comfort zone. But what if you don't? When do you take that BIG LEAP?

There are always going to be people in business that do extremely well. Your perceived competition will challenge you by their success and either demotivate you or drive you to achieve better. I'll share more on focus later in the book, but many entrepreneurs step sideways, not forwards, because they care too much about their competition. Imposter syndrome is a bitch!

There's a tendency to be so passionate about our business that we live through it. We sacrifice our lives, opportunities that are in front of us, and magical moments with our loved ones. I see so many business owners burn out, working so many long hours, trying to juggle everything themselves and literally get to a point where they're exhausted. In some extremes I've seen them physically suffer breakdowns and illnesses that FORCE them to STOP!

The warning signs were there and they ignored them. They were so persistent in craving success, more opportunities, taking on new clients and in doing so, they forgot to serve themselves first. They forgot to take time for their most invaluable asset in business.

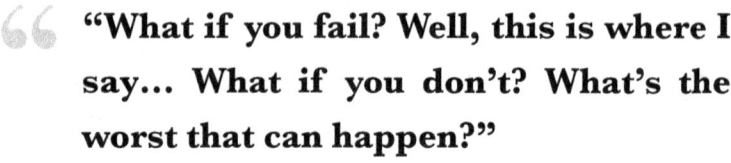

"What if you fail? Well, this is where I say... What if you don't? What's the worst that can happen?"

— *KELLY VIKINGS*

Guess what - you are NOT alone! Everyone feels the same. If they don't then who are they kidding?

The truth is you're only likely to fail if you're not ready, you don't have what it takes, you don't have the support around you and you don't have resources to support you. Failing isn't all it is set out to be! It actually isn't that bad. When life has served you with shit storms... what does it leave you with? Strength, tenacity and a bucketful of life lessons. It's the same in business. Fail, fail fast, learn! I can say this because I've failed many times. However, it hasn't stopped me. It has actually made me the sum of who I am today.

So whether you're considering taking that first giant leap or not, there will be a driver, a reason. Your divine purpose to take that LEAP OF FAITH.

- You've experienced something, realised you can bring a solution and help serve others. You feel you are unique.
- You're fed up with your corporate role, after spending many years working your ass off for your employers, and for what?
- You desire a flexible working pattern that supports your lifestyle.
- You've been made redundant and decided now is the time to start your own business.
- You've always wanted to be your own boss and build your own teams.
- You've realised your dream is to build a virtual, digital business, with global limitless connectivity.

There are so many factors, and I'm really looking forward to sharing the incredible short cuts, the smarter, more enjoyable ways of building a business, with the many lessons I've learnt through my business failure and building my business online.

I wouldn't have it any other way: a free life, on my terms, taking the highs with the lows, being a business leader, is the only way for me. I LOVE it. I lead my business from my heart, a place of love and harmony and know you can too, but the reality is that for whatever reason you've chosen to take this path or are living it, your life transforms. It's a new world.

Make sure you remember to have fun along the way!

I just want you to know what you're signing up for. It can be a tough path, but it will be the most rewarding. In the following chapters, you'll learn how to ensure your path flows and is realised with ease, ensuring that you step forward with confidence, belief and have your eyes WIDE OPEN!

It's about being prepared to really dig deep at times. Success tests you like no other.

Are you ready? Have you got what it takes? Your life will transform in so many ways. Have you got what it takes? Are you ready?

This book will really give you these answers, with guidance to really understand the foundations of building a business. Don't forget I know what it's like to have an idea, however crazy it may appear to others. I had no one advising me for many years whilst I was growing my first business. I literally started my business from the kitchen of my rented house, whilst I was a single parent to two young boys. Almost thirteen years after setting up a hugely successful business, I also experienced it crashing around me and losing everything. I started a new business after failing. I focused on building an online business, instead of a traditional office set up with overheads and teams. It's a completely different ballpark.

I'll be sharing the vital lessons I've learnt, even preparing you for the WHAT IFs. If your ideas don't work? If your launch doesn't get the success you initially wanted? The REAL truths and even some of the toughest lessons I have learnt through business failure and what's followed, from that as I built back up again.

Time to remove the BS, to be prepared, to do business in a NEW way that aligns with your true-life path and divine purpose. I believe this book will ultimately save you so many costly lessons in business, which, whether you're just starting or already running your own successful business, may just prepare you for some of the things entrepreneurs and business owners don't often talk about.

Are you ready? OK, let's begin!

YOUR UNIQUE DIVINE BUSINESS CODE TM

*T*his chapter is all about you, as I touch on one of my signature programmes;

The Divine Business Code™ and how a vital part of this programme is about discovering your unique Divine Business Code. Also, I'll talk about how to identify your TRUE superpowers, how they support you in your business, how vital it is to listen to your inner guidance and intuition, and how to tap into an endless fountain of confidence that will absolutely drive your business. At the end of this chapter there's a free 30 day programme. Which supports you to step into your ultimate power, which is found on my website.

Your unique Divine Business Code™

Have you ever seen someone who looks like they have it all together and everything's going their way and in doing so, you've felt a pang of jealousy? You still feel pleased for them and underlyingly you know they've worked hard for their success. Yet, you see them effortlessly create win after win and wonder what they're doing, that maybe you're not?

Have you ever had a conversation with someone who wishes they could be more like you? An employee that wishes they were an entrepreneur with their own business maybe? They see you - your life - and they wish they had a small part of what you have? They're clearly unhappy in their well-paid job, which they've had for ten years, and they see your lifestyle and wish they had that freedom.

By the way, I've felt and experienced both of the above emotions. Jealousy and regret are natural; what we see is often the iceberg effect. You see what you want to see. You believe what you want to believe. Often, it's only the tip of the mountain. I will guide you to see your position from as many different perspectives as possible, not just leaving you believing what you think you see at the top of the mountain.

I want to gift you the knowledge of how it can really be in business - how you can use your own superpowers to guide you to your incredible life and business success.

"Your divine destiny calls you!"

Now is not the time to be paying attention to what others are doing. You've no idea what it took them to get to that level. Maybe even the hardships they faced. Celebrate their wins and know it may be your guiding star to illuminate a roadmap to where you wish to be. Smile when those who observe and make judgements of you, have no idea of the sacrifices it has taken you and celebrate YOUR wins. You're doing this, you've got this and step by step, no matter what, you're crafting your own destiny. They may not understand or support you, but you're driving your own life path and that's incredible! You're brave, you're strong, and you're resilient. You absolutely deserve to celebrate your own WINS. Remember, you never know who you may inspire along the way.

One thing I know to be true is that we are each on our very own unique entrepreneurial journey. Everything starts with you; it always begins with us. We'll only ever shine as bright as the energy we send out. It'll feel harder, things won't flow, and life will not flow with ease if you're not playing to your strengths, your passion, your purpose and the very reason you were born, it will feel much tougher.

We all have a life path, a divine destiny and if we aren't living it, life will 'force' you towards it, over time, in the right direction. If we ignore the signs and sit in our comfort zone or play small, we'll live out a mediocre life path and never play out our true potentiality. Possibly living our life with regrets and lots of what ifs...

I encourage you to discover what you were born to do: what is your life path? We look at this more in Divine Alignment because there really is nothing like the super energy you charge at when you're living your true path. Your heart sings, you're on fire, you are grounded, connected and everything you touch turns to gold. It's incredible.

Before we go there, trust me, you will want to! Let's discover some of your divine qualities.

Take time to work on this if you haven't already. If you think *I'll skip this because...* No excuses, this is for everyone because I can guarantee it would be a mistake to rush through this book.

This is YOUR time to sit still and recognise what you're made of. Before you answer the questions, I want you to just sit with them and see how you feel.

What comes naturally? What do I LOVE to do?

This first question will identify what aligns with your heart space. I've worked with people who have a real passion for doing something that's become their hobby, because they see a far bigger financial vision and their passion doesn't generate the income to substantiate their dream lifestyle or business. However, there will be characteristics or elements of this passion that may fuel their real love for something that would align them to their life path, in a way that brings fulfilment and financial security.

What do I wish I had more time for?

Seek for the answers to what you 'wish' you could do more of. There will be something that really resonates on a far deeper level that literally leaves you in a state of pure flow and feels super easy. You may not realise it is a super skill because you're so used to applying yourself to this task, yet to others it could be their worst nightmare. The thing your soul craves to do is often the thing that brings your soul its most joyful moments.

What gives me the most satisfaction in the work I do?

We all go into business with a vision: there's always a reason, a WHY! As I previously mentioned, I've interviewed hundreds of business owners and leaders and there is, without a doubt, a 100% genuine reason that set them on their unique path. It's no coincidence they're all about the feeling they get that comes from deep within the soul. That reason is always a feeling - a satisfaction and sense of desire to make a difference, to be a catalyst of change. I'm asking you, what is yours? What feeling does being/living/breathing in your business create for you? Recognise this and enjoy the feeling it sparks. This is your driver, your driving force to being YOU.

What I find really easy in my business or current role is…?

Often, you will wish this is what you could focus on ALL the time, but sadly business isn't like that. We all have to become proficient with all things when we start and build a business. Running a business isn't just about that one thing. What do you find comes really easily to you? Is it creativity, communication, numbers, sales, marketing? Or are you more analytical, maybe analysing the finer detail, copy, graphs, branding or maybe creating websites? We all have something, or key areas, we excel at naturally.

What frustrates me?

If I said that nothing will frustrate you in business, I would be lying to you. There isn't a single heartbeat that doesn't feel frustrated at certain times, or even undertaking specific business activities. There's always something that will frustrate you. What are the very things that feel out of alignment? What do you avoid? What feels like really hard work and you wish you could either outsource or not do? It will be interesting to see how many items you list here.

What has the potential to trigger me?

By trigger, I mean more than what makes you irate. There's a line you reach, and when you go over it, you'll be pushed over the edge. You will feel extra sensitised and often these triggers will bring out a side to you that you may wish to avoid, as they leave you feeling angry, disappointed or shameful, or maybe even guilty about a past situation or belief. It is ok: be truly honest with yourself. When we identify these triggers, we can choose to work with them.

What do other people see in me?

How do others see you? It's time to look past your own feelings and realise how others see you. It's vitally important you communicate, and your actions align with, your business intentions. If you're a Confidence Coach, yet you don't ooze confidence, there's a disconnect. You may even want to ask your close connections privately or do a post on social media and see what people write about you, on the last question. This can be very revealing.

Time to answer the questions.

I want you to think about your answers to those business focused questions and even take your time to journal them.

List your top three to five things that come to mind. More if they come through.

- **What comes naturally? What do I LOVE to do?**
- **What do I wish I had more time for?**
- **What gives me the most satisfaction in the work I do?**
- **What I find really easy in my business or current role is…?**
- **What frustrates me?**
- **What has the potential to trigger me?**
- **What do other people see in me?**

This should not feel like a difficult task, if it comes from a place of truth. Let me explain how these will really help guide you to discovering your divine qualities.

What you're left with is a clear idea of what you're naturally aligned to doing, what you enjoy committing your time to, what you gain the most personal reward from doing and what you're naturally gifted at doing. Along with that, you learn what doesn't align with you, what past experiences or beliefs can potentially come at you and how other people may see you.

If you go against your highest self, by living a life out of alignment and running a business out of alignment, it certainly will feel hard work and it's going to mean you have to build a huge team to support the areas that don't feel natural, and all sorts of negative emotions will play with your mindset. It makes the chances of business survival a lot slimmer and leads to a very unhappy existence.

What you can do is change your direction by making choices that guide you towards your divine destiny. I believe if you're not stepping towards this path, you will experience warning signs, and if these signs are avoided the universe will shift you, sometimes by serving tough lessons until you're finally on your right path. This is tapping into a deeper meaning, a deeper level that will fill your soul with everything it desires to feel truly aligned and live consciously guided by purpose.

Being divinely guided by your soul and trusting in your inner strength, desires and guidance will lead to an abundance of opportunities that will create an energy that is off the Richter scale. It is an incredible feeling and a truly phenomenal path to live, breathe and honour every day. You truly feel grateful for everything that you attract and every opportunity that comes your way. I will talk about this more in Divine Alignment™.

Can you imagine how life would look for you if you weren't taking this step towards your power, or you wished you could do something and never did? A life with regrets. I often ask my clients the following:

> "If you could see your future self ten years from now, what would you be doing differently to today?"

Visualise her, see her, talk to her...

If you had that opportunity, what would she be doing?

How would she feel if she was exactly where you are today?

Would she thank you for living with truth, courage and conviction?

Would she wish you had made different choices?

When we live through our experiences, we sometimes experience pain. It can feel as if we are being punished or that we have done or are doing something wrong.

The Divine Feminine is Mother Earth. She stands for evolution, and we realise that no pain is a sentence or punishment and that she guides us. She is purpose driven and sees your truth, your life path. When you trust in her she shows you how to move forwards, how to turn all those hurtful experiences into lessons to grow, evolve and become an embodiment of love, truth and light.

She does not seek perfection, she never judges, and this can be a powerful reminder that we are exactly where we are meant to be and nothing ever happened without a reason: it was a path we took. We are limitless, we are free to choose any new path and we can live our truest, highest self, choosing to step into our true power, our divine destiny that eagerly awaits us.

This chapter is about discovering your highest self and unlocking your unique Divine Business Code.

All my work that supports my clients to work uniquely with you, supporting you and your business journey in every way. Everything begins with you! We're all completely unique and have very different life experiences. I never put anyone into a 'one size box fits all' because it NEVER does.

I just want to take the opportunity to thank you for reading this, for taking time to work on you, and for investing your time in the most precious asset you have, you!

CREATING YOUR VISION, YOUR PURPOSE, YOUR WHY

I genuinely wish that everyone could be crystal clear and understand how to clearly articulate what their vision is for life and their business. I ask myself constantly, WHAT is it that stops them? Fear of not achieving everything their heart desires? Fear of sharing it because of not wanting to sound big headed or irrelevant? It genuinely saddens me that so many incredible business owners have no idea what they're working so hard to achieve. What is their driving force, their purpose, their WHY?

If you're one of those people that right now are reading this and thinking... yep, that's me... then now is the time to change it. Right NOW!

Or you could be reading this and want to shout, no I DO know what it is I want for my life and business. I challenge you to say this in fewer than four or five sentences with utter conviction and belief. It is here most business leaders stumble. They fail to articulate in a way that really connects to their most precious identity, their soul, and often they say out loud what they believe they should be saying, NOT what connects deeply to the magnificence of their being, their heart space, their soul.

I've also recognised through studying different human design modalities that I happen to be one of the crazy ones that comes up with many concepts and ideas and this is why, for me, helping my clients to create theirs not only comes very naturally but also effectively manages my desire to constantly create new projects. Detailing your vision is complex. It does not take away how important it is to convey your vision or how clearly each area needs to be communicated powerfully.

I want all my clients to know that what creates inner peace, what really motivates them, is the core of why they do what they do. I want them to smile, to truly BELIEVE in their power and vision and be able to articulate it in a way that is truly powerful and really resonates with their clients, family, friends - everywhere they shine their light.

Your vision is so powerful. It opens the gateways to everything you think, do and become. Most importantly it sharpens your mindset, which is your driving force that guides your business daily, motivating you to do the things you do or don't need to do such as the decisions you make and the influences you connect with. It gives you the joy you have even whilst doing the things you don't always prefer to do.

Vision is the catalyst to success in both your life and business, both your inner and outer worlds. They combine to create the life your soul searches for, your Divine Destiny. It aligns you, steers you through challenges, drives you forwards every second in every day.

A good friend and inspiration to me, Vikas Malkani, the world's No. 1 Wisdom Coach, said to me in an online event I organised the following words, which really echoed my own thoughts:

> **"Vision is the art of seeing the invisible, believing the impossible, realising the intangible."**
>
> — VIKAS MALKANI

For me, this is the true spirit of an entrepreneur, a business leader. We must create a vision of what is not real, of what is not yet created and visualise that image in our mind's eye.

We know exactly what it is we are committed to, determinedly and persistently chasing, creating and delivering. We see, feel, BELIEVE in it so much that we sacrifice many things, taking courageous risks. We contribute by turning up daily, often investing our personal resources, challenging ourselves, managing a million balls, often taking action on NEW business strategies we believe will create a tangible outcome, from what was sparked in our minds, which we see clearly as our vision. Our reasons that support our WHY!

The more clarity we have and the more succinctly we use compelling words to describe our most precious of visions, the more we can condense and be not just committed, determined and persistent, but the more we can create a specific strategy that allows us to work smarter and determines the quality and outcomes of our results.

This is why having a clear vision and a strategy (mission) to support your ideas and create a tangible outcome not only gives you a strong foundation to operate from, but it also feeds into your daily productivity and performance and steers every decision you make to create the outcomes your heart and your soul desire, guiding you to live out your Divine Destiny and achieve your aspirations and dreams.

Our vision does not have to be driven by monetary gain, wealth or unimaginable success. Not everybody wants to create a business that feeds their ego, feeds their financial hunger. For some, this is about realising their desires and a love of serving others, which personally rewards them with so much fulfilment, seeing their own clients truly achieve their own versions of success through fulfilling their visions!

The sadness I experience with many business leaders is that they lack confidence to align their life outcomes to their business strategies. Even worse, they don't execute them, which results in continued disappointment and feelings of frustration, fear and deep disappointment. This is where many of them seek support from outside sources, like a coach or mentor. If this is poorly guided or mis-sold, it can lead to even more personal disappointment or business failures, which is why taking time to discover the right coach or mentor for you is crucial to your business success.

Again, the word alignment comes to mind here! Not only should you discover a coach or mentor who truly listens to you, but also one who supports you to achieve your totally unique vision and has the right skills supporting you to achieve them.

It's at the beginning of everything I do with my clients: to understand their VISION, their driving force that motivates them, their reasons why they're doing what they're doing. What is it all for? When my clients don't quite know how to articulate this, I take time to create a Vision Statement that determines exactly what they want to achieve and how we can create the relevant business strategies to support them to do so.

So how do we create clarity of our vision?

Let's begin by answering these specific questions that help you to form a Vision Statement for your business. What this allows you to do is really create a North Star that guides you towards achieving your vision and being able to communicate this clearly, connecting with your clients on a much deeper level. It really is very powerful. If you take time to do this, I know you will be steps ahead of many entrepreneurs and business leaders. Recognise that laying the foundations to your business isn't always shiny, but the time you invest is all about building a strong foundation to grow from.

A leader will only ever establish a loyal following and create a connected audience when they share a vision that their audience believes in, buys into and trusts. This is why having the answers to these questions is so powerful.

Why do you do what you do?

What are you helping your clients to achieve?

What is the outcome of your work going to achieve?

When you first answer these questions, you will most likely reel off a huge list. The next step is to try to bring this back to three key words in each question. You do this by prioritising what feels aligned to you the most. Prioritise what gives you that sense of real satisfaction and belief, confidence in what you do and why you do it.

So now ask:

What are the TOP three drivers that drive your business?

What are the TOP three outcomes or solutions you wish to achieve through your work?

You want to create a Vision Statement that is crystal clear, that motivates you emotionally, is realistic and achievable, but also really connects with your audience on a deeper level. The best way to do this is create your vision from your heart space and deliver directly from source, soul.

Therefore, when you say the words you create, they flow with conviction and ease. To really condense this down and give crystal clear clarity, positioning and strong key messages to your clients, followers and audience, try to complete this following statement.

To help you, here's **my** Vision Statement.

My Vision: 'To empower women in business to step into their Divine Feminine Ultimate Power.'

Here are some further examples of major global companies' Vision Statements.

Patagonia

 "We're in business to save our home planet."

Tesla

 "To accelerate the world's transition to sustainable energy."

Amazon

 "To be Earth's most customer centric company; to build a place where people can come to find and discover anything they might want to buy online."

I'd like to encourage you to do the same. This is part of your power statement.

It's your vision and it connects with your soul's desire, with all you wish to achieve. It also connects with your audience deeply and clarifies what you do and the reason why.

Try not to confuse a Vision Statement with a Mission Statement. Often the two are written together. I will share all about this in the next chapter. For now, what's your vision?

Why not download the 'Create Your Vision Statement' resource from my website?
It is a free tool I've gifted to help you create your very own version of your Vision Statement.

One thing I've learnt is that the more aligned, the more passion fuelled your creative ideas are, the more personal reward it serves you. The more purpose driven, heart centric your ideas are, the more likely you are to consciously commit to them.

All of these create a cocktail that drives you forwards, achieving the greatness you truly desire.

You would not start, if you did not believe.

You would not continue, if you did not believe.

Time to stop playing small, stop hiding in the shadows.

Now is your time to really shine, discover who you are, and exactly what you are here to create in your lifetime.

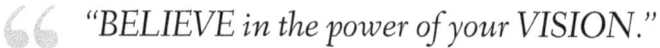 *"BELIEVE in the power of your VISION."*

DEFINING YOUR ULTIMATE MISSION

Having now created your Vision Statement, a powerful vision is what really steps into the future of what your business wishes to achieve and guides you to your ultimate potentiality.

What is your mission statement and who is this for?

Your VISION is your North Star guiding Business Success.

Your MISSION is what drives and delivers your Business Success.

Now we turn to really breaking this down into creating your mission, i.e., knowing how you really want to stand out and achieve everything your heart desires. PLEASE don't think you can achieve everything in one day, six months or even your first business year.

Remember, the biggest of achievements take time and require you to be consistent, patient and backed up with a bucket load of belief!

Your vision goes a long way to fuelling this, especially when you practise visualising daily. But, what about your mission?

A Mission Statement should be communicated to ALL those who represent your business. Not just clients, but those who work in it, and even your suppliers. It communicates what the purpose of your business is and why it exists. It may evolve as your business grows, whereas a vision is something you tend to evolve into. So don't worry if your mission statement changes: this is evolution and growth.

Knowing your business's core purpose focuses it on what it aims to deliver. It's really important to understand your business position, i.e. your niche or to understand your competitive edge. So, you can really challenge your existence and share what makes you unique.

Niche is what makes your business unique; competitive edge is what stands you out from your competition. Both give your business a competitive position.

It should be a statement that, like your finished Vision Statement, is condensed into a short paragraph that delivers impact and is communicated daily. It will ultimately underpin your business values and every person you grow in your team will equally embody your mission statement in all the work they deliver.

It takes your creative energy and ideas, that may seem so far away, and bridges the gap, giving you more confidence to take that leap of faith in yourself. Also, this is for those who need reassurance and tangible proof, those who do diligence and want something to evidence their creative ideas, whilst taking them from ideas to reality. The more business experience we have, the more we realise there are greater risks involved and so business strategy is not a bore: it's a foundation, a framework that really identifies and supports your business growth.

This is a Masterplan at its early stages and yet it is one I don't hear enough about. Some people believe they have to be an organisation or large company to create their Mission Statement. That's absolutely NOT true!

Some questions to maybe help you unlock your creative flow and get really specific:

What is it you do?

Who do you serve?

How do you serve them?

What are the outcomes your clients will achieve?

Or maybe these sentence starters feel more relatable:

We provide...

We offer...

We are a...

Our clients...

Here's my Mission Statement:

My Mission

'To ensure every woman, from all corners of the world, steps into her heart space, discovers her truth, connects to her Divine Ultimate Power, to evoke blissful **Divine Alignment™**. Building strong business foundations discovered in the secrets of **The Divine Business Code™** creating Divine Strength, Success and Wealth.'

Here are some further examples of major global companies' Mission Statements.

Spotify

'Our mission is to unlock the potential of human creativity by giving a million creative artists the opportunity to live off their art and billions of fans the opportunity to enjoy and be inspired by it.'

Google

'To organize the world's information and make it universally accessible and useful.'

Whole Foods Market

"Our deepest purpose as an organization is helping support the health, well-being, and healing of both people - customers, team members and business organizations in general - and the planet."

I'd like to encourage you to do the same. This is part of your power statement.

It's your mission that drives you and your teams, and shares how your business chooses to deliver its vision. It also connects deeply with your audience.

Again, try not to confuse a Mission statement with a Vision Statement. Often the two are written together. In the previous chapter you will have written your Vision Statement; now it's time to share your Mission Statement.

Why not download the 'Create Your Mission Statement' resource from my website? www.kellyvikings.com
It is a free tool I've gifted to help you create your very own version of your Mission Statement.

DIVINE BUSINESS BLUEPRINT

So many times, when working with my amazing, incredible clients, I see exactly what they were born to be doing, yet for whatever reason they initially don't have the confidence, belief or even realise their unique gifts and superpowers and it holds them back.

Damn you, past!

Yes, it's almost definitely something that was done to them, or that they experienced, or that they've done that creeps into the present version of themselves and suffocates the beauty of what could be their highest, truest future self.

In 2019, after my business failure and everything I had experienced emotionally, physically and mentally, I had to find the courage to 'try' to take some small steps forward.

My partner knew I needed a break, to get away, so he booked me onto a course in Tarragona in Spain with some ladies I had been creating some working relationships with. I remember feeling like a fraud. Why should I be going to this? Why did I deserve this? Yet, as we flew across the ocean, the clouds below us and surrounded in some really positive, high vibrational energy, I began to let go and have some fun for the first time in what felt like years. Being in an arena full of sensational energy, watching speakers over three days talk about 'The Power of Success' and sharing the fundamentals to becoming a Global Leader gave me goosebumps. I knew I had it in me. It was so exhilarating and lifting!

Yet, returning to my home, I felt the weight return. Every street I drove past, or shop I went into, my past was following me. It was crippling me with shame, fear and guilt. Then I was brutally attacked by the press for trying to rebuild my life. For daring to build a new business... I mean, come on! I was not earning much money at all; I was stepping forwards. I was trying and, mentally, physically and emotionally, I was absolutely frozen. I know these kinds of judgements can destroy us. They get in deep and freeze us; they stop us from stepping forwards into our future.

A Divine Business Blueprint is a business plan. It is a mission broken down into actionable steps and if ANYTHING or ANYONE steps in your way, ask yourself, who is paying the price? What price is there at risk?

I love listening to music, lyrics, words with real meaning. I can recall hearing these words and I clung on to them for some time. They became my daily mantra…

 "YOU'VE BEEN TOO STRONG - FOR TOO LONG.

NEVER FEAR YOUR PAST, YOU'RE NOT YOUR PAST,

ALWAYS PRESENT YOUR FUTURE."

I genuinely believe we're not our past; we must learn to let go. It takes bravery to do so. Remember why we are doing this. Why we've decided to create our own destiny and start or grow our own business. We must learn from ALL our life and business experiences, take away the invaluable lessons and instead of living in the 'HARD KNOCKS', learn to let them go, and take the lessons with us that we can use in our future, especially to help others.

So this is where your past, present and future are in fact a sum of everything you were, are and will become. Embody this and embrace it. Honour it, because if you don't, you won't create new space to grow, you won't move forwards freely, and you won't step fully into your Divine and Ultimate Power.

I'm so hugely passionate about women standing tall in their truths. Owning their mistakes, their lessons and sharing them to break down these illusions of perfect lifestyles and businesses. There's NO SUCH thing! Everyone's experienced knocks and the more we share, the more we break down barriers and give women, incredible women like you, the freedom to be exactly who you are, to really shine your light and in turn encourage, inspire, and empower others.

You see, it's not just about liberating and standing and owning your truths, it's about total alignment. When you share truths, especially at first, it feels hard and uncomfortable. You don't want to always go back and sit in the past - and why should you? But to be true to yourself and others is so powerful because you recognise YOU in this process, the real you. I will share more on this in Divine Alignment in Chapter Seven.

What I will say is this: too many women are showing up as who they think they have to be to gain success or be seen as successful, or they are wearing a mask, hiding who they really are underneath because of a lack of confidence, shame or imposter syndrome. They pretend that everything's ok or will work out, when it won't. They live in circumstances that truly do not serve their soul. They are surviving, drowning in painful, hidden emotions, none of which will serve their health, self-love or how they truly show up to the world.

Turn fear or imposter syndrome on its head, make friends with it, learn to use it as a driving force to who you will become.

To be successful you don't have to be a certain way. What success is for you is completely different to everyone else. Masculine energy is important, to have balance between feminine and masculine energy. Like yin and yang, it's important. However, too many women are walking in high masculine energy spaces, which is not good for their soul.

Being YOU is unique. There is no one the same, who's lived the same life experiences and has the same business knowledge. No one!

> "I wish I could wave a magic wand for women around the world, to step into their own true divine destiny and shine their divine feminine energy every-where with pride."

Avoidance stemmed from fear stops action and can be internally crippling. Yet, if we avoid it, not only does it chip away at our soul, but it magnifies the lessons learnt when we finally have the bravery to face whatever it is that's holding us back from taking action. Our comfort zone may feel like an easier choice, but F-M-L it's a painful and pretty dull existence!

> "We get one lifetime; we don't know how long we have in this human body experience. Time to make every second count!"

There are so many lessons to be learnt. The biggest one is recognisation of our identity, who we truly are and being confident, brave and connected enough that it aligns to our outside world. For some this is pretty scary, and others may try to hide, but the universe will find a way to shift you. Circumstances will lead you to discover the realities of why you are here.

We must ensure our internal world is deeply connected to our heart space. We step into our Divine Feminine energy to honour this. We come from a place of truth and compassion for others and know in our hearts our business is here to bring us self-fulfilment, a lifestyle of quality, and the desired outcomes that align with our future selves as women. We are aligning the outer worlds to live out our divine destiny.

A Divine Business Blueprint takes your vision and mission, underpinning the essence of exactly who you are today and drawing a map, giving you clarity on how to navigate from where you are to where you wish to be. It will incorporate both your life and business goals. Not just your business goals, or else, being really honest, what's the point? You may even have an urge to be a game changer and fulfil a lifetime desire to create a legacy to leave an imprint upon the world. It combines everything, giving you clarity of all the things you wish to achieve, setting your intentions and allowing you to work towards them and track your growth.

You will know what it is you wish to bring to the world in terms of your business ideas. With this will come your business model, online, offline or hybrid.

If you're a coach or mentor you will have your business model broken down into signature programmes, events, and other products and services that will attract your audience to you.

If you're a healer or practitioner, you will have your range of programmes and service offerings.

All businesses have an indication of what they wish to bring to the world, which iss underpinned by their vision. Then it's about creating a scalable and sustainable business model that's viable and brings you the income and lifestyle you desire longer term.

For many coaches this is about scaling up and creating one to many programmes, or masterclasses that incorporate working with more than one person. Like retreats, these can be an invaluable way for people to learn from each other and collaborate and connect on a deeper level.

For some it's about working one to one and building a business in this way. Either way these are the building blocks to creating your ascension business model and Divine Business Blueprint.

Of course, there are the challenges of setting fees and working to time sensitive frameworks: i.e., if you wanted to start your business to give you freedom and flexibility, you may not wish to be working sixty hours plus a week! It must work for you; it must feel aligned to your core vision. We all have the same hours, minutes, seconds in any given day. Each business leader will feel compelled and be aligned to their own unique Divine Business Blueprint. My biggest advice is to go with what aligns to you, not what everyone else is doing.

In order to win new business, the next steps are of course to know how many clients you wish to attract, and how you wish to prioritise your marketing and PR Strategies.

To do this, you need to understand fully who you're marketing to and how you can communicate with your clients effectively.

When I work with my clients, we map out ninety days, or a more intensive twelve months Divine Business Blueprint. It's invaluable to plan ahead, ensuring they know confidently each month what they're working on and towards. Building resilience and setting realistic goals are so important, as of course is an understanding and confidence about financial forecasting. This makes sure they know exactly what they're working towards and they identify any short comings. All of this is vital to building your own unique Divine Business Blueprint.

What I find very frustrating as a Business Mentor is that for many business leaders and entrepreneurs, unless they've run a Company, a tangible business, they don't work enough on their business and this crucial guidance system that lays their business foundations is forgotten. Many new entrepreneurs are playing at business, and yet are putting so much pressure on themselves, but still don't have that clarity to draw from. Then they question why business is so tough, why they haven't made any money, and are often investing thousands of pounds on courses that don't support the one thing that holds everything together like glue. Or I see business owners write their ideas down, but fail to consider their vision and why they're doing it all. They lose their initial driver and then wonder why their business didn't work. This is why so many businesses fail in their first three years.

Even worse are business leaders who THINK they have it all sorted! 'Yeah, I'm ok. I know how many clients I need and what courses I'm launching this year, how many members I want in my online membership, how many sales I need to project.' BUT they fail to work out their profits. The actual profits and they don't analyse their cash flow, or even worse, don't even have it in their business plan... at all! #TRUTH!

It's like having a baby; we aren't taught this. We deliver a baby into the world, and as parents, especially new ones, we do our very best to nurture and protect it. We invest our time and all our energy into being the best mum we can be. No one prepares us for being a parent. We may bring past experiences with us. We may even read a book! Who knows, but we don't get a MANUAL on how to bring up a baby and be the 100% perfect parent! This doesn't happen.

It's the same in business. We start a business with our WHY. We do our best, investing thousands of hours, often doing things we've never done before, like social media marketing, live videos or creating courses. We overlook the **BUILDING BLOCKS** of finances because we're so focused on other areas that grow our business. But if we have blind spots and we undercharge or we invest in too many courses and don't make enough... we run out of money! Or what is visible to the outside world is growth and wealth and actually it's all illusion; the business owner is making zero as they are shedding their money out the back door, so to speak. I see it all the time, which is why I say don't always believe what you see!

There's no operations manual, systems or processes that FIT one business, because just like each business is unique, each business operates differently to accommodate and fulfil its business owner's desires and ambitions.

I host Divine Business Strategy Days working with business leaders who want to scale up their business. My mission is to ensure I give them the tools that fundamentally support the business owner's lifestyle and unique life circumstances to achieve their ambitions to grow their business. We address their blind spots, ensuring they have crystal clear clarity and really take their time to work on their business, not just being sucked into it!

Being a Divine Business Mentor, I also work with a number of modalities. I am spiritually guided, I work with Divine Feminine energy, and Lunar and Numeric energies. Many of my clients work with them too and discover how incredible it is to build their framework embodying these ancient teachings into the businesses. One of the most incredible ways to work in alignment and work to our strengths is by using the Power of Numeric Energy.

My trusted, good friend Jo Soley from Bizology®, who's also my exceptional mentor, helped me to incorporate Numerology into my own Divine Business Blueprint. I've featured her in my book. Jo explains in her own words how Numerology and her Bizology® can support you in your life and business. I adore her work and the incredible connection it has given me to really trust in the power of embodying Numerology to support my own business success, but also to recognise who I was on many levels and confidently embrace that. I invited Jo, as one of my mentors, to share her work with you:

USING NUMERIC ENERGIES IN YOUR BUSINESS – JO SOLEY

Bottom line – Knowing your numbers increases your numbers!

Thank you, Kelly, for asking me to write an insert for your book about using numeric energies in business. By way of introduction, I'm Jo, I use the powers of numerology to help business leaders elevate their business success using numerology.

Numerology is a well-established discipline, similar to astrology but instead of looking to the stars, it looks to numbers. Numerology is used by celebrities and CEOs across the world as a way of harnessing the subtle energies that are all around us. Numerology is as old as the hills. Emperor Nero is associated with it. The Egyptians used it in the Hieroglyphics. The Ancient Greeks used it. Pythagoras referenced it in terms of the religion of numbers. It is quoted in the Bible; the Kabbalah is heavily influenced by it (although a different system). Music uses numerology in relation to strings and tones.

BUT it is as NEW as the next decision that you are going to make!

Numerology grants access to higher-level business solutions. Understanding and connecting to my numeric energies has been pivotal to my and my clients' business success.

It has helped me to approach all that I do from a position of strength and it has given me a fresh perspective on doing business in the 21st century.

So, let me share a little about me.

Over the years I have done a lot of 'work' on me and studied different modalities, some resonating more than others. However, learning who I am through the lens of numerology - finally things made sense.

So how does it play out? I am working with the energy of the Life Path number 1. I have a lot of 1 energy in my numeric chart, my Life Path number is a 1, the first initial of my first name, J, is a 1. My first name vibrates at a 1, etc, etc. That is a lot of 1!

1 is about directness, leadership, innovation, individuality, independence and entrepreneurship. There are spectrums to the energy of the numbers: at one end of the spectrum 1s can be selfish and make their life all about them; at the other end of the spectrum, 1s can sometimes be selfless and 'people pleasers'. I know I have certainly been like that in the past!

Why do I connect with it so much and how has it helped me?

The balance for a Life Path number 1 is to put their head down, mind their own business, get on with it, not worry about what others are doing and from that place, serve. This is the M.O. that I have now adopted... and it is working!

Life Path number 1 does not like to be told what to do. They need to be self-employed, independent, and can be innovative in business. To be honest, I was not being very Life Path 1 in my business (I was being very 2 – the power behind the throne and helping others run their business) and that was not working for me. I now appreciate that my Life Path number is just that, very much part of my life, my life story and my destiny.

This information has been so incredibly useful to me, that after extensively studying the subject and integrating it into my business I now spend all my time helping others not to be square pegs in round holes. The foundation of numerology is the concept of uniqueness; it is a discipline that recognises every person and every situation as unique. This is its real power and value. One size does not fit all and there is no magic formula in business. Bizology shows you how to align to your life purpose.

By using these energies in business is how I help many of my clients – including the lovely Kelly!

So where do we start?

YOUR LIFE PATH NUMBER

Your Life Path number (also known as the Destiny number) is THE single most important number in numerology. It is created from the numbers in your date of birth. You cannot change this.

Your life path is your initiation into what you came to do and become – Your Destiny. What you are destined to do here on earth. Understanding your Life Path number really helps you connect to what is possible for you and your business. When your Life Path is explained to you, it will resonate and feel right, as you already know it. The trick is, are you working with or against it? And if against, how is this working out for you?

If we are working in the negative of our Life Path number, you will know about it! Your life will not flow or work for you and you will not feel peace in your life. Instead, you will feel stuck.

But there are better times and easier times to do things...

YOUR PERSONAL YEAR

We work in nine-year cycles. Personal years start on your birthday and end on your birthday and are related to what you are currently working on. Knowing which personal year you are currently in helps you work with the vibration of the year and its energies. It is always the right time to do the right thing but there are better times and years, easier times and years to do things. Working in alignment with our personal years help us 'go with the flow...'.

You and I know that people do business with us if they like, know and trust us.

Numerology helps you like, know and trust YOU.

Understanding your numeric energies helps you move forward, delivering powerful insights that can really help you to show up more effectively in our business. Discovering and working with your numeric energies can help you to improve your creativity and productivity, develop better client relationships and increase profitability.

If you would like to connect with Jo, do reach out to her. Her Facebook business community is incredible Bizology in numbers. I would highly recommend Jo. She transformed my life by sharing my personal numeric readings, and I know she can for you too. I live my days, weeks, months and years all in alignment and with huge trust and insights; it's very powerful.

THE TRUE ESSENCE OF YOU

Hopefully, by now you'll understand and see the huge value in taking time to really work on yourself. Some people may not, and they'll even question, what's the point?

Sometimes it could be very difficult to find the right person, coach or mentor to work with and trust to help support and guide you, investing in this united partnership.

I loved my horses. I've had a few over the years. Quin was without a doubt my absolute favourite and my last horse I will ever own. I have him tattooed on my back. He was extra special. We were deeply connected, and we knew each other through our breath, seated riding position, and had complete trust and love for each other. Towards the end of his days, I knew he was getting older and needed veterinary treatment to help him. He also required physiotherapy and deep tissue healing. I invested in this to hopefully help him recover. Certainly towards the end, the expensive cortisone injections were to help alleviate the pain he was in. If you have ever had an animal, a real SOUL partner, you know the importance of these treatments and you would not (in my opinion) question them, you would invest and believe in them.

Yet so many business leaders fail to invest in themselves! They literally question the many reasons WHY NOT to invest, building up a barrier with excuses:

- I don't need to see a coach or mentor
- They cost too much money
- I don't know someone I can trust
- I don't have time

The list goes on. By the way, I'm not trying to sell coaching or mentoring services here! The fact that I live with one is irrelevant. The fact I'm a mentor is irrelevant too. The point is this... Why do some (not all) business leaders question investments in these skilled therapies for themselves?

The very fact of the matter is this - YOU are the heartbeat of your business.

You are the sat nav that navigates your business.

You are the engine that drives your business.

You are the decision maker and person responsible for every aspect of your business.

You are the ONE person that leads your business to its outcomes.

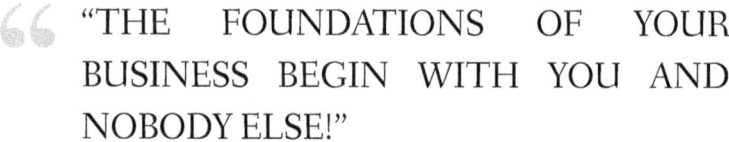 "THE FOUNDATIONS OF YOUR BUSINESS BEGIN WITH YOU AND NOBODY ELSE!"

So, how do we ensure we build 'Miracle Foundations'? Like an elite athlete, we build a team around us, that builds the very best principles to work from within, to facilitate the best possible outcomes in the external world.

It's often taking that leap of faith in ourselves, doing something that stretches us beyond that shitty fear barrier, moves us from our limiting beliefs zone through and way beyond our comfort zones. This is NOT as easy as you think. Seriously it isn't!

When you look at a TOP Athlete you only see the tip of the iceberg. When you look at someone who's achieved what you are wanting to, you only see the 'current' article as I discussed earlier in my book. You never see the shit storms, the bucket loads of persistence, the multiple failures or losses, the sleepless nights, the investments they've made in themselves, to create their Miracle Foundations.

So, now we have got that out the way. What Next?

Well, having never had a Business Mentor in my previous business until the last year, what good has that taught me?

Having not met my partner till one month before everything came crashing down, what good has that taught me?

You may not have the resources to suddenly invest in working with a coach or mentor.

I know how that feels, seeing everyone sign up to courses, programmes, events and feeling I was unable to.

OMG, it was so frustrating and made me feel so unworthy. Let me tell you now, MONEY is NOT your worth! You can let that thought disappear immediately.

However, several of my clients and connections invested in themselves, invested in courses, programmes and events, and came away totally back to square one, money down the drain. They suffered a real setback in their mindset and confidence, feeling deflated and back to square one again.

I've done it. I sold belongings to claw together the money to go a course which was the shittiest course I've ever attended. Needless to say, I don't follow, work with or respect that mentor and would never recommend them to any of my clients. This behaviour and these poor ethics HAVE to stop.

What it has taught me is, there are some incredible coaches and mentors out there with courses, programmes and events that are delivering extraordinary value. You don't have to sign up to them all, and always do your diligence on the expert delivering them. Do not get easily swayed by marketing, scarcity and emotional mind games... fear of missing out! It really is not worth it. I have even been caught out by being friended until I have bought a course, then that 'expert' went off radar. Isn't it interesting what lengths people go to? I guess what I learnt was that we all have to discover this for ourselves, and in the longer game true colours always reveal themselves.

What you can do is gain a shit load of clarity from designing your life on your own terms by levelling up on creating your own Divine Business Blueprint. This will give you a bucketful of inspiration and confidence to take that initial leap of faith in yourself.

To really help build Miracle Foundations here are some vital ingredients...

- **Commitment**
- **Consistency**
- **Discipline**
- **Energy**

You've probably read many more or have heard this before, but for me these are very much still KEY to my daily success in building my Miracle Foundations. Here's why...

- **Commitment**

I categorically can't do anything unless I'm fully IN! I'm committed! One step forward and I know this is my full commitment. Having this attitude towards my work means I don't ever step in and just give up. If I stop, it's a decision based on tangible evidence to support the reason why I've stopped.

Having your own degree of commitment will keep you focused on your vision, what you're trying to create longer term in your business, and drive you even when the path gets tricky, or something or someone maybe tries to side-line you!

When I'm building my foundations, I'm committing to my Divine Business Blueprint and so must you.

- **Consistency**

Doing something once is good - giving it a try and stepping beyond your comfort zone. Do it repeatedly and it becomes your comfort zone. Then what? A NEW level awaits. If you do something and move on to the next shiny object and do something else, you may weaken your outcomes.

Learn to be consistent. Try a LIVE 365-day FB Video Challenge. See your audience grow and support you. Do four posts a day for three months. See your audience grow organically. DO it once or twice. See NO impact!

If you want to create bigger impact, being consistent will unlock the door for so many more opportunities. The same goes for your daily actions. Visualisation, time blocking, working with numeric energy, walking and grounding in nature to revitalise your soul; the list goes on. I think you get my point, but trust me, this doesn't just happen, you also need:

- **Discipline**

THIS for me underpins your Miracle Foundations in a BIG way!

To have an extraordinary life takes disciplined, focused daily action. Discipline is the easiest one to hide from, yet is the most productive.

THINK athlete, ELITE Pro! They train in every weather. They have the self-discipline of an ox. Their desire to achieve their ambitions fuels their personal productivity and performance. They take full responsibility for this themselves and for their actions. They may have all the magical foundations in the world, but when the door is closed, they go home and they train in their home gyms. If they don't have discipline, they can find their productivity and performance compromised.

Discipline is not just turning up; it's living and breathing your discipline. Also very important, especially for women, is our:

- **Energy**

This is something that fascinates me... Human Design. In our genetic makeup and unique DNA, each and every one of us is completely different. We may have built up muscle memory, I liken that to my personal resilience. It has been built up and has muscle memory. When I get knocked down, I am able to bounce forwards quickly previous past experiences to help me move forwards. Yet as soon as I use tech for too long, or forgo an early night, I'm done! My energy dips. We are each unique through our own human DNA.

We all have an idea of what our energy levels feel like with the lifestyle we lead, yet is this way of operating serving our souls? How many people do you see trying to build their business and they appear to have it all? Then you see them looking like they have had four rounds in the ring with Mike Tyson, or they post, **"I've had to take time off social media because I've felt so exhausted."**

Wouldn't it be amazing if we could truly understand our Energy and instead of repeating these frequent, unhelpful patterns, we nurtured them? We then live our lives and grow our businesses in a way that serves our soul and energises us.

There is an ultimate ENERGY code. Energy transmits: if transmitted at a high vibration, it attracts an abundance of high vibration and positivity, so it really is an important ingredient to respect and work in balance and harmony with, really honouring your soul.

For over three years, I was living in survival mode and failed to nurture my body, honour it and gift it what it truly needed and deserved... to STEP out of survival mode.

Friday and Sundays are days I consciously choose to slow down. By creating divine and sacred space for self, and by truly taking time to practise 'The Power of Pause'

Something I respectfully bring into my week, to create space for reflection and processing the week gone by but also to honour what I'm becoming, and I would encourage you to do the same. See balance and harmony become part of your life and positively impact your inner and outer worlds. So important for each of us to be able to honour this to have the grounded, centred energy to be able to achieve such greatness in our lives.

SUPER CONNECTIVITY

$\mathcal{H}$ere I am right now, jumping right in front of you to say...

> "Connection is THE most important aspect of your life and business."

Then hug you tight, because when I connect, I always lead with love. Global pandemic or not, hugs are welcome any time, any day!

I hear you nodding, hopefully smiling. We all like to feel connected to a loved one, our family, our friends, our communities, offline and online. Connection is that virtual 'hug'. That moment you feel connected is like a silent bond has been written, signifying love, trust and connection.

So let's look at how this helps you to not only grow your business, but grow YOU personally too, in so many wonderful soul fulfilling ways.

Picture this...

You may even have been here before. If not, remember this because I want you to avoid this happening to you. You've worked on many aspects of creating a new offer; you know this is really going to help so many people; you've invested in creating design artwork, or taken hours to create artwork yourself; you're feeling really proud. You've created the name, put together marketing copy, and you're now ready to launch! Your heart is beating fast... You press POST. It's out there: your work is going to impact millions of (Ok, maybe twenty or thirty – it's early days!) people's lives.... How amazing! Then... nothing.

Now, the fact is we all have to go through this, but there is a better, smarter way.

It will not break your confidence and set you back emotionally. We all know what it feels like to experience setbacks.

Do you recognise any of these sentences?

Only three people signed up.

I didn't get enough people into my free challenge.

I did all that work and no one signed up.

That's it: I've failed. It didn't work and it's not for me.

I'm going to cancel this; there aren't enough people signed up.

I need to invest thousands of pounds into a course to learn how to do this properly.

I've invested thousands of pounds on a course and it hasn't worked.

What a waste of money. It's not their fault, it's me.

They were really supportive at first, but no one signed up.

OMG, how am I ever going to make any money?

I GET IT! I've felt, to a certain extent, all of those things and probably more.

So how does CONNECTION and being a Super Connector erase all these emotional feelings and bring RESULTS?

Let me ask you a couple of questions. Be honest, you're only answering to yourself.

How many people are you 'connected to' via social media?

Do you genuinely connect with your audience? Real conversations?

Do you refrain from using your personal accounts for business posts?

Are you too scared to post more than once or maybe twice a day?

Did you answer them? Now another question.

If you are going to change the world...

If your work is going to IMPACT thousands of people's lives...

HOW are you going to do this by starting with small numbers, not getting to know and truly connect with your connections and hiding away, even fearing what other people may think of you?

SERIOUSLY!

The thing is, there's no magical formula, no quick fix. This is why building your business (especially online) takes time and effort! You can't hide. The only person that hides you from stepping out and launching into your friggin' POWER is...You.

Before you dream of selling to thousands of people, before you even consider investing in a course maybe, INVEST in yourself. Connect with your heart space. Feel that confidence, trust your vision, visualise what really connecting with others will lead to. Discover your driving force, feel motivated daily to not 'thumb scroll' but become that person who posts real connective content that powerfully attracts and connects your audience and ignites real conversations.

Growing your audience

Not only will you enjoy social media, but you will build a circle of trusted friends and connections by really committing to growing your audience. These are the by-products, but OMG, they are magical. They are experiences that really help you to step up and leap out from behind your shadow!

If you have 200-400 friends, an inactive FB Community or none, the chances are you're not ready to launch your incredible ideas to the world. Why? Because you'll feel disappointed and your launches won't bring you the results you aspire to.

I don't want you closing the book, running a few miles and hiding away in shame. This DOES NOT mean your ideas are not good enough or that they don't have the power to transform lives. It just means you have to step back before you leap forwards. Remember this is The Secrets of... I am sharing the magic ingredients!

Even if you have an audience of 3k on Instagram, 4.5k on FB and a FB Community of 1.2k, it does NOT guarantee you will be ready to fly off and book your next trip on a yacht to Dubai, buy a Mulberry handbag and sip cocktails in the sunset.

> "Numbers mean NOTHING if you don't CONNECT to them."

Of course, there's a bit of 'extra magic' in this too. If you have an excellent Copywriter, Photographer, Designer, Social Media Manager, etc, etc, behind you, you will see your audience grow exponentially. The caveat is... this will cost you 1-2k a month!

So, how do you start small and nurture, GROW your audience organically?

You really connect to your highest self, and to your vision and mission, and you share from your heart-space, when you do this, you will create posts that connect with your ideal audience, with other connections who will be inspired by you, and with people you inspire. All on a far deeper level.

You share content every single day, and you don't let your fears step in the way. You jump from behind the shadows and STAND up for what you believe in. You showcase yourself and your experiences, you share your truths and your struggles, you share your daily events - the wins and the losses.

You take your audience on a journey, holding them in a space you create with compassion and from a place of no expectation. You bring them insights and advice, sharing your thoughts and feelings. The more you do this without expectation, from a place of love, the more you organically nurture, grow your audience.

The more you do this, the more you WILL attract high vibration, similar minded, ideal clients... connections. It's not difficult; we make it more complicated than it needs to be.

This is why working on our mindset, commitment, consistency, discipline and nurturing, and protecting our energy, is so important. I'll be sharing more secrets on creating some frameworks, and giving you structure to create marketing content later in the book.

But if you recognise and really appreciate the importance of growing an engaged, connected audience first, it will save you a lot of heart ache, frustration, even money on courses, until you're ready.

Learn the fundamentals and get your foundations in order first. Yes, sometimes declutter, remove the numbers envy and build an audience that is TRUE and serves you, and delivers you not only engagement but real friendships, mentors, peers, people who lift you up and support you. Connections lead to so many wonderful, amazing opportunities, and you will discover how.

You do need to REMOVE the 'this is my personal' FB account. That needs to be chucked in the trash bag!

Do your friends, family, work connections want you to do well? Or do they drain you, and don't understand what it is you want to achieve? Have you spoken to them? Are you giving them the opportunity to remove themselves from your contact list? Have you set boundaries and removed them?

I'm not suggesting you wipe your account and have a massive friends and family cull. I'm going to ask you again... WHO pays your bills, who invests in your work, who contributes to lifting you, supporting you?

If you have a blocker, consider what it is you are trying to achieve? Who is hindering this? Why is it such a problem? What can you do to change this? What are you waiting for?

If you're more concerned about Bob, Trish and Uncle Buck than investing your energy into building and growing your audience, you will hit a roadblock. If you invest that time and really connect deeply with your audience, you will see the advantages and many benefits all come together in twelve to eighteen months' time when you do launch your products and you do have those twenty+ sign ups from people you LOVE working with and who enjoy and appreciate WORKING with you!

Now, there are ways by which to speed this up. They do require time and money investment, though. Yep, there's the catch and there's a ton of risk - will it pay off or not?

What I am talking about here is FB ads, lead magnets, free quizzes, and all the free stuff or paid ads that take time to build. Many business owners don't have the skills or resources to pay to outsource when starting out. Then it hits another roadblock. Ads are again based on numbers, so if you pay to advertise to X people, you will grow by X, but are they quality leads, quality clients? I'll let you answer this...

The best way I've learnt over the fifteen years in business is to put yourself out there, connect with incredible people and TOGETHER support each other, collaborate and contribute to working as a collective. This is a natural, organic and hugely rewarding way to really grow personally and professionally.

CONNECTION IS EVERYTHING

Your Clients are not just a) the reason you serve and do what you do, or b) your income stream. If you always think of people as opportunity and monetary rewards, you will soon find yourself scratching behind the sofa for any coins you can find.

> "Your Clients - Are the Heartbeat of your Business"

Now you've got it! Yaaaaayyyy!

I loved writing this chapter by the way. I hope you're finally seeing why your clients are the heartbeat of your business: you in one chamber, them nestled closely in the other. As we continue, you'll see why it's so important to really know who they are, but also to connect deeply with them on a much deeper and more meaningful level.

Without them you have nothing. If they fly away and disappear, you have nothing and all you worked so hard for disappears. Literally, your clients are GOLD to you.

When I see hugely successful business leaders tip over the ego wheel, you see how they treat their clients. I ask myself, 'How do they still get away with it?' I also VOW to never forget what it's like to have nothing, to start from nothing and to share as much as I can to help others, respectfully always putting... **PEOPLE before PROFIT!**

YOUR BRAND

Of all the things you work on in your business, being able to really clarify CLEARLY your brand identity and what it stands for is so important. Otherwise, how do you expect to grow your audience and connect with the right people, who ultimately could be your ideal client? How do you expect them to know you're THE ONE?

If I had twenty incredible, amazing, Kick Ass ladies stood before me and asked each of them to SHOUT out what they did, what they stood for, how they showed up to the world, and what their clients would say about them... can you guess how many would be able to CLEARLY, CONFIDENTLY and with PASSION shout out what their brand stood for? It sounds so easy, doesn't it? Well, I guarantee you, as little as 10-15% of business leaders could answer this so that it rolls off their tongue with real conviction and truth from a place of knowing and utter belief.

It actually frustrates the shizzle out of me; it really doesn't take long to clarify your message! Let's try it together. I want you to be in that 10-15% clear as fudge category, and go out there with conviction, truth, knowing and utter belief in all you do and stand for!

Try this exercise - I would love to hear your answers too.

Come find me on FB or email me kelly@kellyvikings.com

Finish the following sentences:

I am...

What I do is...

What I will achieve is...

Working specifically with...

My clients' outcomes will be...

This is fantastic, but can you hand on heart say it came from your heart space and was concise, not waffly, and you felt passion, truth and conviction in your words? Ditch the sheets of paper, ditch the bullet points: did it really come from your heart space?

Time and time again, I hear the words that really matter and connect with the business leader, but they don't hear it immediately...

I want you to try it again. This time:

SPEAK YOUR TRUTH

SPEAK FROM YOUR HEART

SPEAK YOUR PASSION

Stand up and draw a breath and feel that connection. What comes through from your sub-conscious and connects with your conscious mind when you ask these questions and answer them from this space? Not from what your mentor, your inspirational leaders, your early business leaders said. This is to come from your heart space, the person you are stepping into and becoming.

How did this feel? Did you recognise a difference?

I often record this work on video. The difference is HUGE for my clients. I share this exercise with you too, as a gift to you, your future self, that highest vision you hold deeply within your heart.

I know you can really stand tall and really take this exercise a step further...

How? You may ask! Well, here we go!

If you take this from a space of ONENESS, it changes the power of delivery. It connects to the highest version of you, and it resonates with the one client who, you know in your heart, you can truly be a catalyst of change for. It gives you permission to offer that ONE solution that can absolutely change your ideal client's life!

So, now we talk with ONENESS, giving your delivery of your message a really strong connection and POWER. When you achieve this, you're steps ahead of so many other business leaders. It really will have a huge impact.

Try this next exercise -

ONE YOU - I am...

ONE VISION - What I do is...

ONE MISSION - What I will achieve is...

ONE CLIENT - Working specifically with...

ONE IMPACT - My clients' outcomes will be...

Here is my BRAND statement to my clients. I thought I would share it now, not to interfere with your own words but to guide you if you need to see someone else's. Remember this MUST come from your own heart space with your own words. Don't be tempted to copy!

Kelly Vikings - The Divine Business Leader. I mentor and empower women in business, ensuring every woman steps into her heart space, discovers her truth, and connects to her divine ultimate power, in order to evoke blissful **Divine Alignment™**. They will build strong business foundations discovered in **The Divine Business Code™** creating Divine Strength, Success and Wealth.

I would love you to step away from this chapter, re-write your social media bios, and extend that outwards to your offerings, websites, media packs - all the places you can now fully step into your power and shine. I haven't concluded yet, so before you make a mad rush, continue to the end of our chapter! If you visit my website I have an ebook that helps you to write your variations of bio's, your stories, and your media packs - www.kellyvikings.com

You will want to draw up many examples of your new brand statement so that you can work with it in your short FB profile, Instagram bio, LinkedIn bio, maybe even your longer bios for sending to potential media, PR or podcasting opportunities. The many options will give you different opportunities in terms of character counts. My advice is the take the KEY words from what you create or extend it to include a little more. KEEP that focus of ONENESS.

BRAND - what does it mean?

Our BRAND is not just a logo or our business name. It isn't the awards we win, or the car we drive to and from work, or the clothes we wear on our skin. It's the heartbeat of your business and shows others what you stand for and how working with you is going to potentially change their life or business.

If we went back to when I first started my business in 2007, Personal Brand wasn't really widely talked about or discussed. Then I recall some business leaders embracing their personal identity on their social media bios and taking personal ownership for their position, career or indeed, their own business personal brand. Yet many business leaders would say having a personal brand was like having an ego. Nowadays of course, it's totally recognised and fully embraced that we all have our own unique personality and how we show up online and offline determines our very own personal brand.

Influencers globally have made millions of pounds from this industry alone and clever marketing strategies have been undertaken by global giants, who sponsor these global influencers to service their products and services, capitalising on their huge audiences.

Even now in today's online market, smaller scale influencers are linking, collaborating through affiliation and pushing more sales through the power of personal brands and wider connectivity and in turn reaching wider audiences. It's a very clever way to create more impact, which converts to more sales.

How do you see your Personal Brand?

Not all, but some of my clients and followers still tend to shy away from creating their very own personal brand, sometimes hiding behind their company title. Does it serve them? Will it help to support their business growth? What do you think?

I'll share more on this later on in the book, but right now, the answer is... if you're building an online business, your personal brand needs to be seen. In fact, it must be seen by as many people in your audience, in your wider connections' audiences and in as many places as you can possibly be seen.

People buy people and they can only buy from you if you have clearly demonstrated through your personal brand exactly who you are, what you do and how you can help them, and if they LIKE you and also if they feel they can TRUST you. Otherwise, if they can't see it clearly, how will they know?

An example... Your personal brand supports your business. You're a Women's Confidence Coach. You have a smaller audience. You don't really use your personal FB for growing your business. You have an Instagram account and sometimes post on there.

You don't have a powerful bio. You regularly use FB to identify potential new clients and direct them to your FB Business page. You don't like going LIVE, and rarely share video content with your audience...

How well do you believe you'll be seen?

If your personal FB page has a photo of the forest and your kids, how well do you believe your potential clients will identify and trust in your personal brand? Will they immediately connect with you?

The answer is NO.

You must take note of this. Seriously!

Think of it this way... If you were searching for a confidence coach who worked with women and transformed lives, how would you find them? What would you look for? How often do you look for FB Business Pages? How often do you see your friends' posts pop up?

This is why it's so important to consistently share your brand, your unique personality, with your potential clients. I can't stress this enough. If you go to market with an incredible opportunity, launching a new course and people don't know you, then they don't understand you and they aren't sure if they trust you.

You will have wasted all that time and energy. You'll feel completely deflated and you can spend thousands of pounds on online courses, but if you don't get these business foundations right, BRAND being a KEY part to your success, including personal brand, you'll be wasting a lot of money going round in circles.

If you sense the frustration in my voice here, this is only because if more business owners spent this time working on this part of their business, instead of scrolling on FB, hiding in the shadows... spent less time taking part in FB challenges or online courses, and actually worked on this, it would be a totally different story. This is how important it is!

So, I'm glad we got that cleared up. I'll share how you market smartly later in my book, really having the courage and confidence to share your branding. It really is simple, and you'll love it, I promise.

What are your BRAND values?

I'd love for you to really stop to think about what your BRAND values are. Your brand values guide your business decisions and principles so why not take time to consider how your customers, clients and potential clients may wish to see how you incorporate these into your business?

Here are some guiding questions to help you begin to identify them.

- What values underpin your brand and how does this connect with your clients?
- Write down the KEY words that really connect with your heart space.
- When you think about your business, how does it feel?
- What words describe the values that will always guide you, and the principles in which you will operate?

Create your own BRAND values. I'd recommend short-listing these to your top five.

What are your Brand Promises?

A way to connect more deeply with your clients and share what your BRAND delivers is to share your brand promises. These are very powerful as they resonate and connect more deeply with your clients, instilling trust and integrity.

Let me share mine first. I've reduced mine to five to keep it nice and simple.

My 5 KEY Brand promises

1. I will always serve from a place of Unity, Equality, Inclusion and Truth.
2. I will always lead with Love and Compassion.
3. When serving my clients, I promise to create a space of Alignment, Balance and Harmony.
4. Connection, Collaboration and Contribution will always be the core focus of nurturing my communities, memberships, digital courses and events.
5. I will always pay it forwards and offer scholarships to my clients: a step to building a lasting legacy that supports those who are facing or have faced adversity or business losses.

Now you can see how I've done mine, why not create your own? These can be used in social media marketing or, very powerfully, placed on your own website. They should be written as Brand Promises that you conduct your business by, promising to your clients. Each word must be spoken in truth.

My Brand Values are...

YOUR SUPERPOWERS

There's always something ultra powerful, attractive and incredibly magnetic about seeing a woman in complete flow, in her space of Divine Alignment.

I believe we all have a sense of what this feels like, when we do that 'thing' that is timeless, creates powerful energy and just feels so right every damn time!

For some of us, we're armed with a big bag of superpowers. For some of us, we focus on one thing and we own it, but we all have something that feels incredibly good and deep down we know what that is, even if we're a little humble and don't shout it from the rooftops.

So, let me ask, is your business incorporating your superpowers? Do you get to be in that creative flow or energy space every day? Wow, it feels good, doesn't it! What if you haven't discovered it? What If you're not able to experience this every day?

This is where my signature programme Divine Alignment comes into its powerful force. It is a programme I have created and work through intimately with my clients or is available to work through independently online. It removes everything that holds you back, no matter what stage you are on your business journey.

For now, let's imagine you've discovered it and you're able to not just live it, but work with it daily. This is where you'll discover your unique edge, even if there are thousands of business coaches or online business owners that offer what you do. They will not be you and they will not deliver it in the same way. This is where you begin to carve out your niche. Really own your space. Shine and thrive in it with a 'kick ass' sense of ownership in your lane. This is also known as business positioning.

As a natural born champion of others, a sensitive soul that really connects with other people's emotions, I love to see people doing this. Why? Because it leads to even more confidence, even more creative flow of impactful energy and a real sense of self-fulfilment. This alignment leads to a radiance that becomes a magnet for your future success, embodying the true essence of who you are and connecting with others in a way that creates balance, harmony and Divine Enlightenment. It turns:

Confidence into BELIEF, thoughts into ACTION and results into ultimate SUCCESS!

Carving your niche and creating space, distance between you and your competitors, by creating positioning that resonates with your clients is very powerful. Let me give you an example of someone I have previously worked with.

Lisa Johnson

Lisa began her career as a luxury, bespoke, high end wedding planner that realised pretty quickly she had an innate leadership style, an energy that business leaders were drawn to, and that she could help coach women in business. Realising her strengths and superpowers, Lisa took a leap of faith in herself and turned her focus into becoming a Business Strategist. As her confidence and real lifetime results were coming in, Lisa was feeling her lifestyle was being compromised. This did not align to her values of creating a business to create a life of freedom aligned to her soul purpose.

Lisa identified a new way to achieve the same results for her clients but on a bigger scale, which gave them freedom. In terms of business positioning, Lisa has become a globally recognised powerful brand. She runs many online courses, masterclasses and communities, which have all been built by one thing that clearly positions Lisa as the...

'Passive Income Strategist'

Lisa does not just talk the talk, she walks it. This didn't happen overnight; Lisa evolved and grew into her niche with every sense of knowing. This is why it's so possible for you to do the same. I invited Lisa to share an insert in my book, which you can read in Chapter 13.

We all EVOLVE and GROW our way through success in business!

It is having the patience in all you are becoming...

You have to step in and do the hard work and experience these things first-hand. Don't give up at the first challenge or piece of criticism. Don't be afraid to step into a NEW area to carve a business position. It is evolution at its finest and if you discover it, it opens the door to a whole new world of possibilities, waiting just on the other side of where you are today, right now, in this very moment.

So, let me talk about influence, standing in your truths and sharing your journey. Why is this all so possible and what makes Lisa Johnson's and many other Global Business Leaders' stories so relatable to you? Let me share...

The thing about carving a niche and really owning your superpower is this. Without even realising it, your divine purpose becomes even more defined. With powerful marketing it attracts your audience and because you've clearly defined what it is, they've invested in you; they trust you. They buy into you, your products and want to work with you.

This is the power of our Niche or Business Positioning: it gives us real influence.

Influence to be identified, recognised and create real change and impact in people's lives.

There is one thing to be mindful of, however you may see this, as you surf the internet or scroll through social media. Some influencers use their newly gained 'influential power' to feed their profit before people in 'make me rich' schemes, stopping at nothing with newly gained ego, oh sorry... power! This is not good and people like me can see it a million, trillion gazillion times ahead. It is not ethical; it sends out the wrong message and in today's world, good human who beings are stepping out of 'comfort' or moving out of 'adversity or losses' to try to make something of themselves and work independently, don't always see the bit in the middle, only the end result. They sign up to other influencers' courses thinking they will make it rich quick. It does NOT happen overnight!

Anyway, my point here is, influence is really good if it's used like Lisa Johnson does, just like myself and many good, authentic human beings, that do go out of their way to create change and transformation for the better in people's lives.

I would like to also point out that we can't be the best at everything. If we try to spread ourselves to thin it won't create the desired outcomes we seek. We may lose confidence in our clients, we must know what it is we excel at and prioritise on this.

I know my strengths in business are showing my clients how to start, grow and scale their businesses. Also, to build powerful strategies, such as organic, authentic audience growth, marketing, and business blueprints. I love supporting my clients through my intimate one to one work, group events, courses, programmes and my written and spoken work.

I believe once we know this, we are not searching for answers, but how to improve and refine our offerings.

THIS is key to my own success and can be to yours too!

How do we really know if an influencer is genuine, authentic and real? I think that decision is ultimately up to us as individuals to make from our own experiences. Having learnt the hard way about trust and business partnerships, being diligent is important, which is why as well as positioning, we must really get to grips with sharing our story, our truths. Not only does it give you credibility, but it really is also a unique advantage that sets you apart and builds your positioning and unique competitive edge.

Another fine example here. One of my friends, who is soooo lovely: Michelle Griffith-Robinson is a superhero, a former British Olympic Triple Jumper. After many years of committing and dedicating her life to becoming and being a successful Olympian, Michelle stepped away to naturally become an incredible Life Coach as well as speaker and ambassador for many incredible charities and brands that are close to her heart.

Michelle's story not only drives her, but her superpowers also underpin her new life path and coaching methods. Michelle is such a huge inspiration and has such a big, beautiful, bold energy that lights up the world. By sharing her story, Michelle's clients connect with her beautiful energy. There are so many similarities in training athletically for an event, that you can transfer to real life or business teachings or lessons. Those skills and intrinsic similarities give Michelle her credibility, and by sharing her truths she's walked forward into a new life path with so much joy, confidence and a loyal following.

I realise that whilst not everyone reading this will be a former Olympian and have this incredible back story, I believe you will be able to relate, because the point I am trying to make is that Michelle, by sharing her remarkable life journey, people connect with her, they connect to her energy, her truths. Your audience and loyal followers want to know about you, they want to understand you. When you share your own unique story, you will connect deeply with your readers. What's lovely is that you can bring them on your journey with you and really get to reveal the real you.

I hope this really inspires you to get to connect with your superpowers and own them. This is what stepping up and into your Divine Feminine Energy is about: really honouring yourself and sharing this, shining bright into the world.

 "You are not the same as anyone else; you are perfect just as you are!"

POWERFUL ORGANIC MARKETING

*E*veryone has a powerful message to share to the world. You just need to discover it, step into it and share it with the world to create connection and ripples, then waves of impact.

Think of some of the most Divine, heartfelt, emotional adverts on TV, in glossy magazines, across social media. They connect deeply; they often share such a powerful message that resonates; they make you smile; you may even shed a tear; they connect with EMOTION. This is why Divine Alignment and stepping into your unique Brand is so powerful. Not only does it give you ultimate confidence and reinforces your self-belief, it creates the most connective messaging for your business.

If you have soppy, inconsistent messaging that doesn't deliver simplicity or clarity, or you leave out 'calls to action' and don't ask for new business, then is it any surprise that your messaging isn't working? How do you expect your clients to connect to you? To remember and trust you? To know how to reach out to you?

Let me share my powerful marketing tips that have worked for myself and my clients and will absolutely work for you too. It really is so important to step out from the shadows and shine brightly. Grow your audience first through powerful marketing messages. Experiment with them. See what works and what doesn't work. This is one of the first bricks you lay upon your business foundations. We want to get this right so you can build a HUGE friggin' empire!

Where to start?

I begin with selecting my KEY marketing words. These are the words you will use like ribbons, weaving them throughout your business, everywhere it's seen. They may encompass your brand values or promises. They'll stand out and signal like a bright beacon - THIS IS ME!

As you grow and evolve in your business you may wish to review and go back to these. We all grow and evolve and so your key marketing words may too.

Here are my key words I use in my business:

My Key Marketing Words

Love	Divine Feminine
Strength	Divine Alignment
Integrity	Expansion
Trust	Truth
Courage	Brave
Divine Purpose	Business Warrior
Harmony	Self-Compassion
Balance	Ultimate Power
Community	Heart space
Connection	Sacred space
Collaboration	Power
Contribution	Divine Destiny
Nurture	Compassion
Values	Protection
Success	Divine Wealth and Prosperity

Write down your KEY marketing words. Remember, let them come from your heart space. You shouldn't have to think deeply; they will come through intuitive connection.

The main reason I do this is because if you thread these words into everything you're guided creatively to produce or bring to your clients, they will know, like your brand, that it's YOU!

They'll become familiar with your powerful words and marketing. After all, words are symbols, and symbols are magic!

Creating these links is aligning your messaging to the brand you've created, making it easier and more familiar to your clients to connect in a way that's just so powerful and beautiful it's like listening to music, the sweetest harmony.

It should feel this way for you too, as you write and create your marketing messages. Honestly, that divine guidance and flow is just beautiful. That vibration is what really sets you apart and like a magnet, attracts your clients effortlessly. This is exactly how I see a successful business, like a beautiful symphony...

There's also a way to bring these words together and create maximum connectivity and impact. You can be as creative as you like with this framework I produced. It does apply to social media posts, blogs or even live videos. I would use another framework for storytelling. I'll share that one with you afterwards.

*To make this easy to remember, I use the digits on my hands to create five parts to this powerful formula.

1 - Create Attention and Stand Out!

A title. Make it really stand out. This is after all is your opportunity to catch the attention of your ideal clients or existing clients and say... Read ME! Is this a problem? Are you sharing something exciting? Start with impact to capture your audience's attention.

Some examples:

- When was the last time you...?
- Are you a...?
- Something amazing's coming soon...
- Let me share how to...

2 - Why you?

Sounds crazy but always share who you are and why you have the personal experience or credibility to write this post.

Examples

- I'm a Business Mentor and my clients experience these challenges.

- I've worked so hard to bring this to you. Make sure you don't miss out on taking this exciting new opportunity!
- As a Business Mentor with 23 years' experience, I'm the expert on growing your business organically. Let me share how to...

3 - Connection and Trust

Write your post and draw your reader in with powerful emotional connection. Share what you're talking about: the example, story, expert tips, whatever topic you are writing on. Share the outcomes they'll experience for themselves, with why you are the person who has the credibility and the answers they need. 'The reason I do this is because...': your reader wants to know why they're reading this post, that it's written for them and why you're credible enough to write and share it. This connects and will instil a level of trust, especially the more consistently you share and the more times they connect with you.

4 - The Message

Recap of the experience, the solutions or the benefits and why you're the expert.

5 - Call to Action

Where does your reader go from here? What are you directing them to or what action would you like them to take?

Why don't you try this five-step framework and see the results you get? I'd love to hear from you to see if they work for you. Use this framework below and test it yourself in your next social media post or live video.

1 - Title!
Create Attention and Stand Out

2 - Who are you?
Why you?

3 - What is your story/experience/solutions/benefits that HELP them?

Connection and Trust

4 - Shorter message that recaps

The Message

5 - What do they do next!

Call to Action

Your Story

Your story can be very powerful, sharing a unique narrative that connects deeply and often on an emotional level with your audience and potential clients.

It's so powerful to share your personal journey or story. Sometimes people don't want their friends or family to read this, or they have so little or so much of a back story that they feel overwhelmed or that it's not relevant. I hear all the excuses under the sun and often smile from a place of love. Until I work with my clients because…

> "WE ALL HAVE A UNIQUE AND POWERFUL MESSAGE TO SHARE WITH THE WORLD"

I have never worked with anyone who doesn't. There's always a huge WHY and there's always a catalyst for becoming a business leader. We all have nuggets of inspiration from our past that may help someone today. These are our lessons, skills, strengths and what we bring forward with us today.

I'll share a story blueprint that will help you share your story. If you're like me and have a million, zillion things that you could share, from both life and business, don't feel you have to condense them into ONE page, post or live. Work at putting together many powerful stories that all make up part of your powerful marketing messages and really connect deeply with your clients.

You may feel that fear creep in. What if **X** reads this? What if my **X** reads this? What will people think? This is where you have to make a decision about what feels right for you. Who are you sharing your story with? What messages can you share to inspire others with? Will it connect and help to grow your audience and potentially gain new clients? Those people you're concerned might be watching, reading, commenting - are they the people you're writing for? If they're holding you back, maybe it's time to set boundaries and remove those blockers.

Your business will not grow if you hold back and hold on to negative beliefs or thought patterns... Success will always test you!

1. Where are you today, presently, right now?
2. What happened? What was the toughest point or realisation?
3. When was that big 'moment', possibly your catalyst and driver to change?
4. What are your core powerful messages, often

lessons brought forward, inspirational pieces that really help support others?
5. Why maybe you do what you do today or why have you created your programme or services?
6. Always bring it back to them. How does this help them? What does it do to inspire action?

You see, your story is not just powerful, it's also your foundation and inspiration piece to shine your light to others, showing them there is another way. For me this is to always lead with love and from a place of unexpected service to others.

Try writing your story. This can be many versions with different messages. Sometimes I see people worry they have too much to share, in this instance, very much like my own, break it down and write into daily posts. I have shared my own story over 6 days. It takes the overwhelm out of it & makes it easier for your audience to read & process. It can also be used on social media, live videos, your website and to promote PR opportunities and more. Have fun with this and see what comes through intuitively. Again, always come from a place of truth, and compassion for others.Where am I today? Describe my current life or business position. (Remember you are taking them on a journey. Start from today!)

1. What was the breaking point or the point in my life I knew I had to make decisions?
2. What was my catalyst and driver to change? The breakthrough moment. What will resonate with my readers?
3. What are the biggest core lessons learnt or inspirational powerful messages to share?
4. Explain what and why I do what I do today.
5. Now finally bring it back to them. How does this help or inspire your readers? What can they learn and implement into their lives and what will this give them?

I've shared these because I've seen so many business leaders not share theirs. The ones who do know the real power in inspiring others and leading others. This is what I'd love to encourage you to do to if you're ready to.

Connectivity through powerful messaging also nurtures new relationships with new connections. Even sharing your story as an introduction when joining new communities online can connect you to a far wider audience.

What some business leaders forget to do once they connect with people is to nurture relationships in a meaningful way.

This is why I set up a sacred space, my FB Community:

Divine Feminine - Women in Business

To support women to connect deeply, encouraging women to nurture healthy relationships online and offline. You will develop a loyal support network and influence so many people by creating powerful marketing and using key marketing words, creating a framework that's consistent and sends strong messages to your networks. By sharing your story you'll nurture and inspire a far wider audience that ultimately will nourish loyalty and grow your business exponentially.

Are you ready to create your very own ripples, your WAVE of impact, with the world?

THE POWER OF YOU!

I'm not sure if you realise how incredible you truly are or acknowledge how beautiful you are. Every day you're evolving and growing forwards, even in the moments you feel tested. Our human existence, body, mind and soul is an unconditional existence we began when we began our human body experience. There is no coincidence in you being here today or reading my book and reading these words. For they are meant for you.

You are truly inspirational, beautiful and brave. I want you to recognise that each of us has a divine strength and power within us. We are here for a reason and if we resist, we will not live out our Divine Life Path. The universe may even step in and force you to recognise your soul's desire until you do surrender and live out your Divine Destiny.

I see and feel so much hurt, pain and hiding in the shadows. I know how it feels to have a past that holds you, grips you, repeatedly haunts you. Life was not meant to always be easy. These moments we went through in our life journey are incremental steppingstones towards teachings and lessons and we need these to understand not only who we are, but also to truly step into our ultimate power, accepting and recognising why we're here today.

Living in abundance and creating a prosperous mindset, we must learn to accept and forgive to move freely forwards. Even through the toughest of times, we must understand deep gratitude and attract all the things we desire in our lives. We cannot move forwards freely if we're living in the past, holding on to old beliefs, not learning from previous mistakes or lessons, and most of all not learning new ways to set new boundaries or to recognise what we are here to do, how we are destined for such greatness in our lives.

Do this from your heart space, a place of honesty and always leading with love. You will enjoy a kinder life journey, you will accept, forgive and move forwards both in your own internal world and the external world.

Leading with love is not always about putting others first, giving to others freely, always saying yes to people's demands, hugs, angel kisses or fluffy unicorns! Although imagine a world with angel kisses and fluffy unicorns...

It's about loving YOU first. Every part of you, your past, present and future self. Honouring every part of you and loving your connection to self unconditionally. When you lead with love, your vibrational energy becomes a magnet to your deepest desires. You shine an energy at a frequency that attracts everything your heart desires. It becomes easier to create your business desires, make decisions and grow your audience through your brand identity and client attraction methods because you're showing up as yourself. Leading with love is setting a version of you at its highest, truest self that others recognise, are attracted to and trust. It's incredible.

So, why doesn't everyone just do this? Why is it so difficult? Are you wondering, 'How can I connect deeply with myself and to others, aligning both my internal and external worlds?'

Being really honest with you, it's because it's so much easier to just bumble along with what feels comfortable. It's so much easier waking up and doing the same stuff every day. It's also easier to blame others or let others influence you. How do I know this to be true? Because for forty years of my life, for the most part, this was my truth.

I didn't ever sit in the past. I was damn good at being who I had to be to survive the shit storms and multiple setbacks I faced and overcame. I was friggin' good at hiding behind a mask. Throwing myself into my work and being 'busy' all the time. Hungry for the next win. I was passionate, driven and highly successful. Was I happy, though? I was fixated on nails, hair, clothes, material and financial wealth. I looked happy, but was I really happy?

The answer is NO. I was under extreme pressure. I was at breaking point. I wanted to prove myself… But to who?

The thing is, we're responsible for the pressure we put on ourselves. Unless you have someone watching over you all the time, no one is asking anything of you. We're also responsible for our internal pressure, making ourselves the priority. However, if we're doing everything for the wrong reasons, like trying to prove to others we are good enough or we're doing it through desperation or necessity, then this is not the Power of You. It has to come from you, for you, honouring the real you.

How do you identify it? How did I not know for forty years? Surely that's impossible?

If you don't stop, you don't listen, you don't put yourself first or you hide behind a mask, you will break or the universe will force you to STOP!

This is exactly what happened to me. I will share a quick insight into the month I realised I had no capital and had hit cash flow crisis in my previous business. It's an important lesson to share...

It was May 2018. (Three years before writing this book)

I realised cash flow had depleted. I was scaling up and it had stretched me. I was running a busy office with eight staff; at the time I was a single mum to three boys. Well, I had a partner, but he wasn't very business minded. I had a staff member I was covering for as they were intermittently sick. I was hugely overwhelmed and stretched, hardly had time to sit down, let alone think clearly.

I was negotiating a big land deal, which was going to involve independently marketing 43 new homes for a sustainable developer. They hit problems with the site, meaning unexpected delays. I was also growing a new wing to my business in which I'd invested staff, digital equipment and was trying to train people. Honestly, it was hell. In amongst this, the one lady who was a real strong player in my team became pregnant and was also very poorly. I couldn't have foreseen any of this...

Hope that paints a clear picture.

One night the boys were with their dads. I had told said partner it was over. I was sat alone in floods of tears, like the weight of the entire world was on my back. I had never felt so alone in my life. Everything I had worked so hard for was slipping away from me. I felt a fraud, a fake. I had to start managing my accounts in order to try to work a way forwards and it was killing me. To stare at my bank balance and see nothing through tears was crippling me, tearing me apart inside.

I knew staffing had to be resolved, but how do you do that when you have no money to pay a new member of staff and were making staff cuts? I knew the land deal would come off, bringing more than enough money to clear my cash flow crisis, but that didn't help in this moment. I knew I could try to sell my home and raise capital, so I put it on the market. Yet the length of sale would not have helped an immediate crisis. I asked my family for financial support, but they couldn't help. I felt completely alone…

In that moment I wrote down the following:

I don't want to live like this.

I don't want to be managing money in this way.

I want to clear my business debt.

I want this to stop.

I don't want to keep wearing a mask.

I don't know how to get out of this.

I want to stop my head from hurting and feeling like I'm living a lie.

I want more time with my children, with being able to focus.

I'd love to meet someone who supports me and makes me feel loved.

Until writing this book, I'd forgotten about the words I'd written, probably due to the nine months that followed, during which I was riding a huge wave the size of a tsunami. I thought I'd found a business investor; it dragged the entire length of my crisis out, up until business closure and left me hugely exposed. The business debt far exceeded what it would have been had I just stopped in June 2018. I did EVERYTHING I could to try to save my business. In the end, this led to the closure of my business in February 2019, leaving a trail of destruction. Me in the centre of this clinging on for life, whilst the press brutally attacked me, and I awaited an investigation into what had happened. I shared in an earlier chapter how I wanted my life to end.

One day something gave me a little nudge to remind myself of what I had written in my book. I leapt up and grabbed it, pulling the pages apart to find the words I'd written.

I asked for this to happen. I wanted it to end. I was not meant to continue on this path. The significant extremes and delays with the investor were never meant to happen and only escalated matters. However, if they hadn't, I would never have met my life partner. This was no coincidence and no matter how traumatic the turbulence of what happened was, and how vulnerable I was, I knew I had to take responsibility and accept what had happened.

I never counted on the end, the closure, the many significant losses being my lessons - that my failures would bring the biggest lessons - I just didn't. After another year, I was beginning to have more clarity and becoming almost impatient, as I knew then that I had a choice to remain broken or to stand up and try again. I had no idea what I wanted to do or who I even was. It was here I discovered my truth, the REAL me and recognised how powerful that truly was.

Even through becoming bankrupt, losing my car, our family home, I knew it was part of the process and my responsibility to turn these setbacks into new beginnings, beginning with taking responsibility, accepting and LOVING myself first.

Now you see why empowering and protecting other women in business is so important to me. Why I'm so insanely passionate about my Divine Alignment programme and sharing my 23 years of business lessons, not just the highs, but the lows too. Even the extreme ones through my Divine Business Code.

In my own discovering, I had to discover my 'confidence and belief' and even for someone who thought they were extremely confident and truly believed it was going to be ok, it was not easy!

Confidence is all about experience and knowing. This is why, if you're aligned and serving your soul's purpose, you will feel exuberant and be much more confident. Belief comes from having clarity and direction in business, knowing your why, knowing what you're doing it for and having enough faith, hope and belief in your thoughts and actions that they will bring you rewards.

Is there ever going to be a situation in which you never lack confidence or never have a dose of lack of self-belief? Nope! We all feel these shadows at times. Like the magical unicorn, there's no magic injection that stops you from feeling these momentary pangs, but if you're not testing yourself and feeling these feelings once in a while, you are not growing, you are not stepping forward into your ultimate power.

Seriously, these emotions can be good. If you didn't feel them, you wouldn't care. That's the thing: you do care, so feel through these emotions, know they are for your own personal growth and learn to navigate through them, always taking you forwards, not backwards. Ask yourself, what's the worst that can happen? Take a mental note, breathe deeply moving forwards.

A big part of having confidence and belief is learning to TRUST and letting go of control, which, when you're running a business, is not an easy thing to master by any means. Especially if you're making decisions from the mind and not tapping into your soul's wisdom, your highest self, intuitively. From a place of sincerity, truth and love is where you meet your heart space, the real depths of your soul. Where decisions are truly aligned to your Divine Destiny.

> "The universe always listens; it has a plan for you..."

It's about learning to trust in this and having gratitude for the moments of celebration and joy, to accept and allow for prosperity to come your way regarding the beliefs and daily contribution you make in your world. Try to visualise the forward movements, however small. Trust they will deliver, take daily action and do stretch yourself. Do face fears head on, do welcome them and learn to lean into those moments more without control, more present moments that you allow to happen and unfold. Daily steps from a place of love, led intuitively, will bring you rewards.

Leading with LOVE is also about my five Cs...

Connection

Communication

Community

Collaboration

Contribution

There's nothing more important than connection. Connection to self and to others.

Connection is where your heart space connects with mind; intuitively you create your own thoughts, actions and connections with others.

Communicating is very powerful in business. There are so many ways we communicate and sometimes fail to communicate or to do so appropriately. Communication of our thoughts, beliefs and perceptions allows us to send powerful messages. Of course, if we fail to see the other side, or do so inappropriately, we must learn to work through the consequences.

Community is a space we create to inspire, support and connect with others, online and offline. It serves our soul's purpose, it gives a space for others and if you're spiritual like me, it gives a safe, sacred place where you build trust, support networks and share both life and business experiences. I love building communities; it gives me a huge sense of satisfaction seeing others contribute and work together. I'll mention more about communities later in the book.

Collaboration is just incredible and if we learn to let go of control in business and we collaborate, we can work as a collective with other business owners and see new creativity, new wider audiences, new ways in which to grow our business. This can be so rewarding and carried out from a place of love; it shines so many positively inspiring messages to others. Think WE not ME. This is a way of working together and sharing invaluable lessons and experiences, bringing something totally unique to the world.

Contribution is another incredibly rewarding action. If done from a place of love, it can be hugely powerful to those you make a contribution to. This doesn't just happen; a contribution is something your conscious asks of you.

It demands something from you that benefits others and often is a gift. The more you contribute without any expectation, the more you create a prosperity vacuum.

Some business leaders do this without thinking about it. They grow success and question the powers of the universe. Their very conscious actions that they have contributed, have brought rewards because they gave without expectation and the universe delivered. Contribution for me is always from a place of love, without expectation, but with your subconscious communicating intuitively to your conscious mind aligning with your divine destiny, it's a magnet to quantum success and prosperity.

I would encourage all my clients, and now you, to consider how my five Cs can make a difference in your business. How do they leave a ripple of love and prosperity? Whose lives do they positively enrich and how can you communicate them?

One way is to go back to BRAND and review your Brand Values and Promises. Maybe they will enlighten you with more ideas that you can create in your business offerings.

	How do I or how can I contribute to these 5 Cs in my business?
Connection	
Communication	
Community	
Collaboration	
Contribution	

DIVINELY GUIDED SALES

*L*et's decide and agree now on ONE common denominator... We all desire the security, opportunities and freedom money buys us.

Brilliant, now let's look into our heart space and seek more answers. Do you believe the energy you put into mastering, creating and serving from your work demands a fee? I'm hoping everyone's answered with another big YES!

Ok, so how do you feel about paying for products or services you've purchased? Again, connect and look into your heart space for the answers...

When I ask myself, and I often do, it's a very mixed feeling. It conjures up many mixed emotions and I'm certain it will for you too. It's often when I reflect on the following it brings up clarity on why I felt those emotions. Recognising the past triggers also gives us a sense of how we show up in the world and what we believe is fair for others, because ultimately, what we're triggered by is not *sales*.

It's *how* we're sold to, the experience we receive having purchased a particular product, and also the value that was received. In some instances, where appropriate, it's also the aftercare and quality of the product or experience itself. No one likes pushy sales or random voice notes from strangers asking for a sale before you've even got to know them. I believe we've all experienced the poor tactics of inexperienced or inappropriate salespeople.

I share the above with you so you can reflect on your experiences, and most importantly the sales journeys you'll nurture with your own clients.

Having a divinely guided sales journey is really beautiful.

You'll never worry about the experiences you've had or just thought about with any unhealthy triggers. Why? Because you'll always be guided, trust, and intuitively make the best decisions for you, your business and your clients. This may sound fluffy, but it's not. It's the same beautiful energy and flow you put into creatively designing and producing your products; it's the same on the other side when you release them to the world. It's an evolving process that's guided and when you trust in this, you'll never have to direct message, chase up, or feel pressured to force a sale ever again.

It's a great shame when we see business leaders mis-selling or bringing very poor services and client experiences to the market, and selling because of their recognised global or influencer status names. This is actually a bigger threat to innocent new and vulnerable business leaders, as they don't see it coming.

I've experienced this personally and felt embarrassed that I was caught in this trap. I sold a collection of things to pay for a course that was full of false promises: the course content was shocking! I witnessed the psychological sway of people lining up to pay for mentorship with inhouse trainers, paying out the money on credit that they didn't have, out of desperation for this 'silver bullet'. It's shocking they use their influential powers in this way.

Have you ever been mis-sold to or had a poor experience that left you vulnerable? It's not just online; it's everywhere online, offline, all across the globe. Quite often, bigger more well-known names lose the intimate, personal touch and attention to detail, delivering a less harmonious client journey. This I have seen so many times. It creates a shadow over those who are leading with integrity and it's shocking to see how they continue to get away with it.

I was in sales for over twenty years. I intuitively worked with each unique set of clients' circumstances. I knew the individual needs of my clients, ensuring I delivered and tried my best at all times to make their experiences informed and less stressful. I knew what potential problems or challenges lay ahead and how to work honestly with all parties and try to resolve them.

I share this because it doesn't matter what you do or what you are selling. There's a process and there's more than one person in the equation. There will be easier people to work with, and sometimes of course, trickier people. We will always have a journey to navigate and if done so sympathetically and with honesty, I believe we can navigate a much smoother way forward. We all come away with an experience and we have a duty as a business owner to provide our best to our clients at all times, protecting and safeguarding our own business and energy in the process.

Each reader's business will be completely unique. Think about your own business for a moment. See if you can answer these questions. I'm not asking for a client profile or for you to map out a client journey and all their touch points (touch points are a marker of every single interaction with your client).

I don't want you to get too deep here. You may find if you have four or five different areas within your business, each one may require its own set of unique answers. When I work with my clients, we cover these areas much more deeply, but now for this purpose, these will help you to begin to identify ways you can begin to implement better ways, or ways that deliver a better process than you may currently offer.

What is it you sell?

Who do you sell to?

Is there a current process in place that creates a client journey?

Do you capture the details of your client early in the process?

How many opportunities do you create to maximise any potential sale opportunities?

How do you work to create the best client journey you can that really stands out and offers your client the very best?

If things do go wrong, what do you have in place to help resolve potential challenges for your client?

Also if things go wrong, what do you have in place to safeguard you, maybe your teams, and protect your business?

How do you refine your current offerings and review them to ensure you are always striving for ultimate success?

Your sales are going to be supported with the magnificence of your powerful marketing strategies. However, if you don't support them with effective and quite simple processes, you will not only lack clarity but lack and maybe even knock your confidence too.

Your confidence comes from having clarity, your previous experiences, and a passion for what you're selling. If you're selling a service, but you don't really know what it is you're selling or who to, you will find it extremely difficult to sell anything! It's the same if you're marketing a product to a client and they don't know who you're selling to or what your product is going to do for them: why would they purchase from you?

You have a new programme, and you're so passionate about it; you release it to the market, and you have the most amazing marketing; but you have no audience to sell to and it's your first time. Imagine the potential impact on your confidence if you don't sell.

This is why I'm so passionate about investing time in building your network and audience first. The more times you try things, even if not perfect, the more experience you gain and this really creates confidence. It's important you learn to walk before you try to run.

What happens if you have a product and put it to market and you have no way of grabbing potential client details, no way of tracking its performance, no way of taking a payment?

No systems in place at all. It just wouldn't work. This is why it's vital to ensure your products and services sales processes are managed first and in a way that supports you to work smarter, to be able to refine your offerings and repeat/improve with real confidence, based on results you create and on what works and what doesn't.

Many times, I mentor my clients and they focus so much on their social media and website and new products that they completely miss why, how and who they're actually going to sell them to!

Everyone's selling something; it's just HOW they're selling it that makes a significant difference. I talk later on about onboarding new clients and I cover much more about having systems and processes in place to enrich your customer's experience.

We all have aspirations for our lifestyles, our future and we seek security and freedom of choice. If we have a genuine service or product that we are bringing to the world, we must ensure we have a sales process that doesn't leave our integrity by the side of the road. We must take responsibility for our customers, clients and their experiences.

I asked Lisa to share what her own views were on selling in the online space, and to share what tips she has to help you. We all learn from our own experiences. We all have a choice on how we respond to the good and the bad. We all have a responsibility, a part to play. I was pleased to see Lisa share how she is committed to breaking down these rogue sales patterns and creating a new way forward that's underpinned by integrity and compassion.

Lisa Johnson - Passive Income Strategist.

Integrity. It's one of those words you'll see bandied about online a lot and even using it these days does make me cringe a bit, but I truly believe we need to.

Four years ago, I started my own business online and in that first year I nearly gave up.

There was so much out there I didn't like. A coach that I paid thousands of pounds to who felt threatened by me and so tried to destroy my business online; a Facebook ads manager that knew how to sell to me really well but then produced no results, leaving me with a huge debt and the selling tactics that I was being taught to use - well, let's just say I wouldn't be able to sleep at night if I had.

And so, I decided to quit. I didn't want to be in an industry that felt unethical. I felt like a bank robber who didn't agree with crime! But then a mentor of mine who I trusted said this to me:

"Instead of moaning about it or quitting, change it from the inside. It can only be changed by showing others what's possible."

I realised she was right and knew that to make any kind of change, I'd have to be memorable and do some big things. Like making a ton of money but the right way. So I decided that instead of sleazy sales tactics I'd just grow an audience of people who needed my help in a Facebook group and help them for free for a while.

For five months I went live most days and gave value. I sold nothing. I decided to be a bit different from the coaches I'd seen out there with their perfect unblemished lives and curated Instagram feeds of perfectly sized size six bodies eating quinoa salad on a yacht, and just tell the truth (you're much more likely to see me cramming a Dairy Milk in my mouth than ever see me eat a quinoa salad). I told them about the ways in which my first business had failed at first and what I'd learnt from it. I showed them inside my business so they could see how I'd got there. I was just honest and transparent, and those words soon became part of my brand values.

In month six I made my first six figures in profit. I had decided to sell a course about business basics to the Facebook group of fewer than a thousand people and had a huge number buy. I realised that because I was being real, I had gained their trust and that's what I'd always do from then on.

My business went from strength to strength and just over three years later I had another launch. This time I declared loudly that we would be doing things with even more integrity. We were in the middle of a global pandemic and would not be selling to anyone who we knew would be getting into debt. We would be turning away anyone if we thought there was a better course out there for them, even if it was a competitor's course (I don't really believe in competition anyway). People told me I was mad and that selling meant you have to push people to buy for their own good. But I didn't care. I wanted to show the industry that you could have integrity and still make money. I wanted to have a ripple effect now that I had a big enough audience and change the industry from the inside just as my mentor had suggested years ago. That launch made me £1.7m in a week. I'd proved it could be done.

Two months later I saw a new coach in her first year talk in a Facebook group about how she had told a prospective client that she wasn't the best fit. She said she nearly took the client's money but realised that a competitor was likely to get the client better results because the competitor had such a similar business model to the client. I got in touch with the new coach and asked her why she had decided to put morals over money. She explained that her coach had taught her to do this. I asked who her coach was. It was someone who had been an affiliate in my own launch two months earlier. The ripple effect had started.

And I'm passionate about it continuing. There are so many of us now that want to see a new, more ethical way of selling online and Kelly is one of them.

So how can you have more integrity when you're selling? Here are five quick ways:

- Never pressure sell. That means not trying to get clients to pay whilst on the consultation call with you. Giving people time to think about their decision. And certainly no 'run to the back of the room now' tactics!
- Always be honest if the thing you are selling won't help the client. If you can see the client isn't ready yet, tell them the truth.
- Always put the client first. If someone else you know is a better fit for them, tell them. They can then make a decision with that knowledge.

- Stop using false scarcity. You know the kind of thing! 'There are only five spots left' when you know there are as many spots left as people will buy. And if you tell people your cart will close at 10pm tomorrow, don't suddenly open it up again for a couple of days. Just be honest.
- No lying or exaggerating your revenue figures online. Be transparent, not only about how much of that was profit but also about how you made it. There is no better audience than one that trusts you.

We really can change how the industry works. We're all in it together and we all have a part to play. And I promise you there's nothing better than making a ton of revenue in your business and knowing you did it with the highest of integrity. Even if that word is overused.

GLOBAL CONNECTIVITY, BUILDING A GLOBAL ONLINE BUSINESS.

The greatest thing about building a business right now, in today's new world is that you have the opportunity to leverage the power of global connectivity to build a global business at your fingertips.

There are many great advantages to this, which I'll be sharing with you.

We observe Celebrity Influencers, Successful Business Leaders and their global audiences, their successes being scattered all over the internet, leaving a trail of hope and inspiration to new business leaders and women wanting to create their own online success stories.

I think it's extremely important we don't put too much pressure on ourselves as women in business. Also, we shouldn't believe everything we see: be extremely diligent; have an understanding that one course sold by these influencers will not make you an overnight success in an instant; accept responsibility for yourself and your learning in the process.

What we often see is the final outcomes, the highs, the top of the iceberg. I want you to recognise that success rarely happens overnight. You'll have to work hard and smart to achieve success and keep it.

I'll be sharing my own personal experiences of growing both an online and offline business model, not just the highs, because it's not all about the wins. It's also about the hard knocks and everything in between. I'd like to provide a view from both sides of the perspective.

OFFLINE BUSINESS

Building an offline business seems like a good place to begin sharing insights. You don't need to have a big flashy office; indeed, the pandemic has shown that global businesses can work effectively and remotely from homes, if the business model permits.

However, if you do choose commercial premises, be prepared for office rents, service charges and various other costs you may be able to avoid by working remotely from a co-working space or home.

A majority of business mentors, coaches and therapists work from home and do not feel the need for an office or a high street location. What having an office does is give you a flagship to your enterprise. More credibility and potential walk-ins to your business. It can also give you a private space for meeting with clients. Of course, you can still gain access to global connectivity online and an office, expanding your enterprises flagship or ships, giving space for potential teams, local, regional or national expansion.

Having had both offline and online premises, I have to say in today's world of uncertaintity not having the commitment to commercial premises is an advantage. It will depend on the type of industry you are in as to whether there is a requirement for commercial premises.

ONLINE BUSINESS

Building an online business excites me most, especially having had a physical office for over twelve years. The benefits it's served me have been invaluable: the costs, remotely connecting with people from all over the world, the flexibility and freedom, without being committed to substantial overheads, fixed staff and pressures of having to run an office.

An online business model has many similarities to the 'core model' itself: the business plan, business brand, marketing, development and sales. Scaling up and sometimes back a little, both have their similar twists and turns, it's like a piece of beautiful music, they play out a similar tune. However, regarding the talent, staffing aspect and recruiting, hiring teams is absolutely more challenging. You're not meeting face to face and you're trusting staff to work to certain standards and operate to your business expectations. Trusting your teams to be more cohesive.

To be fair you would have this potential threat in an office environment, though, were you to recruit staff and they didn't have the talent they declared they did at the beginning of their employed contract. I have experiences of both.

It's apparent there's less control when remotely hiring teams, and this to me is where you must hire with eyes wide open and make often difficult decisions quicker working remotely. There is more flexibility as outsourcing to remote teams is mostly on a monthly basis, allowing you to grow your business with flexibility and speed.

I love building and empowering teams and when you get to this level, you will discover the other side of being an employee, to employer. It is an eye opener. One thing I have been so grateful for is mostly having exceptional staff and teams of experts to outsource to. In building an online business you will never scale unless you build a team. It is inevitable. Find the best talent and really look after them, they are crucial to your business expansion and growth.

Global Limitless Connectivity

The great thing about focusing on building an online business model that connects to limitless global opportunities is that your mindset and focus shifts. It's without a doubt a lot harder to be seen in a bigger audience online. You will have to be committed to being consistent and to differentiating yourself, and be prepared to work really hard to grow your audience.

I mentioned earlier how many business leaders were trying to develop their brand without clarity, and spending hours creating products and services yet not having the audience to sell to, leaving them frustrated, not producing enough leads, and their sales resulting in not enough income, struggling with their mindset and often giving up.

It's often not their ideas and creativity; it's the fact that they have not built an engaged audience yet. They compare themselves to the highflyers; they do not tap into their own unique energy and identity (Divine Alignment); they don't have a comparable large audience to sell to. They can't afford to build up their business, they have bills to pay, they're constantly juggling, often a part time job or trying to build their business whilst holding down a full-time role.

This is so hard to keep and maintain focus, especially if this person has a family to work it all around.

I know this so well because I've been continuously working hard now since September 2019 to build my online business. I have gathered a real insight into what the online business industry is like and have discovered who I can or can't trust. I have also learnt what works and what doesn't and the amount of work you have to do to break through if you're building an online business model as a coach, mentor or therapist. Without my previous business experience it would have been fundamentally a lot harder. It has been a huge learning curve that's for sure.

Many business leaders during lockdown turned to the Global Market. They turned to people that have achieved greater success who have the knowledge from which they could learn how they could scale their businesses or grow quickly with impact to make money from their ideas and products or services online.

It's been an incredible experience learning the One-To-Many business model and I've seen, with my own eyes, the results and authenticity of how this can work for some business owners. What I also see is that it takes time to grow your audience and sometimes you'll have to overcome setbacks when your launches don't quite deliver the results you'd hoped for.

The common challenges are audience size, product itself, brand, marketing strategies, or launch methods; often it is not the business model itself.

One-To-Many takes coaches, mentors and business leaders that would typically be working 1 - 20 clients weekly, to scaling up significantly and creating courses online that create a semi or passive income stream.

This does not work for everyone. There is still a place for intimately working one to one with clients, and often courses that are built online are not always completed and longer term could devalue the work you deliver. I work intimately with my clients knowing intuitively what works for them. It is about what will encourage my clients to grow and take inspired action, never leading to overwhelm, and supporting and encouraging them every step of the way. Everyone is different, as are their business models.

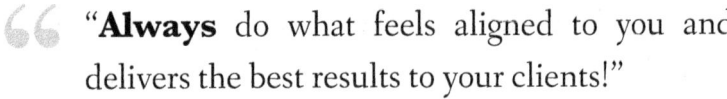
"**Always** do what feels aligned to you and delivers the best results to your clients!"

There are many ways to incorporate passive income streams and to scale a business so you can let it make money for you, turning your financial assets into passive income streams. Of course, property is one of the most popular passive income streams. I won't go deeply into this subject, but I am passionate about ways entrepreneurs and business owners can elevate their financial position and claim financial security to live out their biggest desires in life. Longer term life vision plans are so important to seeing what we are working towards.

As Warren Buffett says,

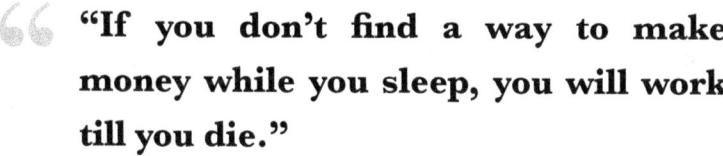 **"If you don't find a way to make money while you sleep, you will work till you die."**

I love this quote because he's so right and with the world at your fingertips and limitless opportunities to do so, there's no reason why you can't achieve this.

MIRACLE FOUNDATIONS

Make sure you're working smarter in business is a line that I often cringe at, but I know it's so bloody true. I had to start from rock bottom, like so many women, and started my business with an idea and a desire to create my successful business. I do feel very blessed. I had thirteen years of my previous business experience, creating, building and scaling a very successful business. Yet many women in business start like me but have little or no experience, and how they do it just inspires me!

I recognise there's so much we wish we'd known or decisions we wish we had made earlier. Mistakes in business cost money and time. Growing an online business model will take a lot more determination and commitment, that's for sure. Make sure you're ready and relentless in your approach, although 'turn up every day' means every day, not every hour! Maintain a healthy, balanced approach.

One thing I wanted to invest in was having a business mentor and initially I felt so deflated because I didn't have the funds but yet I wanted to learn from those who had made it.

I was desperate to work 'smarter' and discover all the available shortcuts, to implement these into my business and begin to make serious money. I know that's how many of you may feel right now. In hindsight, my situation gave me great insights into the online world, influencers, coaches and mentors - not only the results they were having, but equally how they consistently showed up as individuals. It revealed some truths, it gave me time to study who was worth investing in when I was ready, and those whose BS I witnessed and as a result, stepped away from.

It's so important to try things out, to refine and review your work, your connections and have a good oversight of what's going on in your industry. The online world can feel so noisy and a lot of people only share what they want you to see. There are a few people proclaiming to put people first who were not; they are more wrapped up in their own egos and making money. However, there are some incredible opportunities to find: do your due diligence and homework on these mentors, coaches, influencers and see if their credibility and how they show up is consistent. People evolve and do change over time and what they once were isn't always how they are today, so please understand this also.

Discovering a mentor or coach who will support, guide, listen and give you all you need to help you grow your business forwards is essential. Now I'm working with some of the best. I absolutely adore having somebody I can confide in, learning new ways, smarter ways and implementing them into my business and I love sharing my own entire working experiences together to support women like you.

Just for the record, who I am online is exactly who I am offline. Just maybe a little crazier at times, but that's normally after a glass or two of G&T!

So, find a mentor or coach that's further along in their business journey than you, who you trust and can relate to, who can give you all you need to step confidently to that next level. Decide if you need one to one or group coaching or mentoring. This is so important when you are ready and can afford to. You know it will be the best investment you'll make for both you and your business, not forgetting the benefits to your clients too.

Business Model

The first thing to work on is your Ascension Business Model. This sounds like it's a scary, mammoth task while in fact it's not. I wrote my first business model on the back of a napkin, because it came to me whilst I was drinking coffee in Starbucks. It does not need to be anything too complicated. It will evolve as your business will over time. Think of a pyramid...

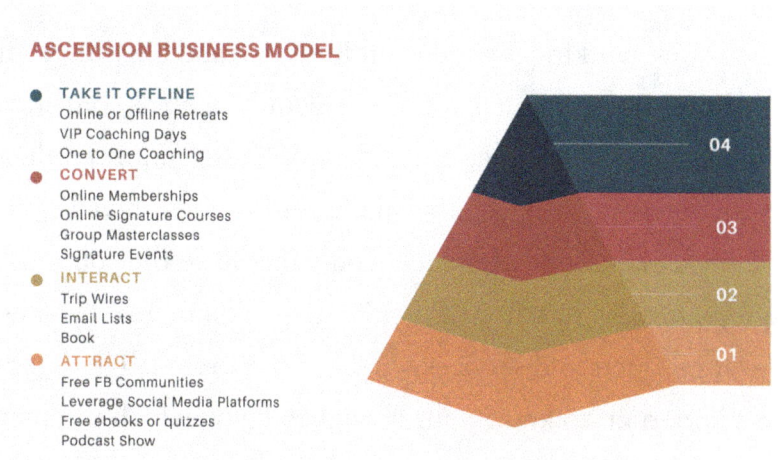

This is Divine Alignment at its best, creating a beautiful journey for your clients.

Essentially, what you're doing is considering the services and products that can be offered to your clients and placing them into levels. As you can see, the bottom is where your free products or services are going to attract the majority of your audience.

From here, as you go up the levels you'll see positioned your other products and services that will demand a higher fee. Be careful when using a lead magnet or free gift to help grow your audience that you are not giving away an item you may be able to sell passively as a low-ticket product that sells and is a great way for your clients to start to work with you.

As you're working towards building trust and aligning yourself with your clients, you'll see your audience convert to clients and this matches the pyramid. It also confirms where your focus is, so if you're building a business model that's solely a one-to-one approach, you won't have the courses or programmes. Equally, if you're an e-commerce business your products and services will be incorporated. That's why it's important to know your clients, to know which products are in high demand and to understand the fees you can attach to them. You'll still be able to produce an ascension business model.

If you're new to business, you may not have all the answers immediately and that's ok. You can grow and work with specifics when you have them. It's important to know and understand your business model though. The more specific you are, the clearer your vision is and your mindset that supports it to grow a defined business that aligns to you and your clients.

Social Media

What structure do you have to support creating impact online? Social media has a variety of purposes. It gets you seen, which will grow your audience. You need an audience to sell to. It allows you to share your credibility and powerful marketing messages. It allows you to grow communities. It can also be great fun. You'll connect with people you may choose to collaborate with. It gives you a global platform to be seen, heard and attract some incredible people. I've already talked about your brand identity and credibility and why it's important to be consistent, but what structure supports you most?

Remember **Image, Title, Content, Call to Action**!

Do bring live videos into your social media. Be patient, grow your confidence and show your personality with your audience. I know it can be scary but if you have a Global Business and you want to see results, you have to step out of your way and go for it.

Have structure to your posts. Vary them and make sure you use social media platforms that work for you. The way to do this is to discover your clients and follow them. A great social media strategy identifies the work you're delivering to your audience and making sure you're preparing them for your next month's launches, events, products, programmes, etc.

Be creative and have strategy to ensure you tick all the boxes. I'll explain in a moment but do post however many times you like in one day. Don't worry about what people are thinking: "She posted five times today." Do what feels right for you. If it's five times a day, you're showing up consistently, you're being seen and that's what is important, especially when you're growing your audience.

This is an example of how having a system and structure will help support you with your social media. It works really well: the trick is to repurpose content you've already written and update the imagery, titles and keep that fresh approach. If you save your posts on a Word doc, maybe even Google Drive, this will make life a lot easier. I'll talk tech shortly but take a look at this and see how you can create your own social media strategy.

Weekly Social Media Grid
Guided Moments of Inspiration & Divine Creativity

Approx Times	8:00 hrs	12:00 hrs	16:00 hrs	18:30 hrs	20:30 hrs
Monday	Q	LV	BDM	G	I
Tuesday	BDM	I	G	Q	S
Wednesday	Q	S	BDM	CP	Q
Thursday	LV	I	S	Q	BDM
Friday	Q	S	BDM	I	LV
Saturday	LV	CP	I	S	G
Sunday	Q	JC	I	S	S

Social Media GRID

Q = Daily Quote
BDM = Business Development - Connecting with your ideal clients
LV = Live Video
I = Info Graphic specific to your industry, business model
G = General - Sharing your journey, with your ideal clients
S = Social - Sharing your FUN and insights into you
JC = Sharing your FB Community

*If Sales i.e., in Launch Week - DO use your BDM opportunities
Or swap some Infographic posts for SALES

FB Communities

Building a community is not for everyone. However, if you're posting onto a business page and expect this to create fresh leads, you'll be better off investing your time growing an online community or other creative ways.

I LOVE my online community. I've had lots of experiences building equestrian, running, women in business and entrepreneurial FB business communities, all with their own purpose and unique audiences. They can be great fun. However, FB has changed a lot over the years and the algorithms have often affected the growth and engagement of communities, which is why I will talk about building an email list to support your growth too.

Like the structure you have for your regular posts on social media, which can be altered for LinkedIn, Instagram, Stories or Reels, FB Communities need a structure too. Write a plan of action. What is it you want to achieve? How many times are you going to post daily? Is there a daily/weekly theme? Are you encouraging your audience to engage with you? What do they take away from being part of your community? Maybe you can encourage them to become ambassadors or partner up with someone to create a partnership and combine arms to create a vibrant, thriving community.

It's important to have structure and consistency. Don't be scared to make changes; it's your community. If you have a poorly engaged FB community, maybe consider closing and starting over again. If you're unhappy, it's also ok to try something else, maybe move away from what you were previously doing. It's an evolving process. This is your permission to create the community that fills your soul with happy beams, because communities can be amazing places!

Marketing

Social media is just one of the areas that creates growth and impact when you're building your online business. There are many other ways to really be seen and they don't have to break the bank. When I didn't have much money and wanted to share my truths about my business closure, I began to speak across FB communities, online events and on other business owners' podcast shows. This is a great way to get your voice out there for free.

Once you begin to feel confident and you've established your brand, your story, and have more profit to invest into your business, working with a PR expert, who can really support you to create media and speaking opportunities in the press, is gold dust. It's a great way to be seen, to establish yourself as the expert in your industry and most importantly, to share your message, vision, story and ENERGY with the world.

I understand speaking isn't for everyone, but if you're like me and see yourself stood on a stage speaking to thousands, maybe millions of people, you have to begin somewhere. Honestly, speaking to one person or thousands is communicating your story with force. A PR expert will help you to communicate your story or message effectively and powerfully. The first time will feel scary. This is where 'big girl pants' work a treat. Breathe, believe and do it, because once you've done it, you can do it again and again! Trust me, it won't feel so scary the more you do it. It isn't for everyone, I appreciate that, but if you have a desire to create HUGE impact, this is your next step.

Also, don't be afraid of creating your own opportunities. Creating podcast, speaking, PR or Media opportunities don't have to break the bank. Of course, it will depend on your time and connections. You can, however, begin to create opportunities independently and if you have little time, make a decision to have teams to help you. I see the importance of creating these opportunities as you can widen your networks, your audience and that can be a catalyst to business growth, longer term financial rewards and creating real IMPACT.

Website

I'm fed up with hearing, "I have to start my website" or, "I have to wait to finish my website before I start my business." OMG... Let me clear this up with you right now...

You do not need a website to start a business, secure clients or to start making profits!

You can start a business, work with clients, receive an income, even create online courses or programmes and sell them, BEFORE having a website. You can build an email list, create lead magnets and a sales pages BEFORE having a website. A website is like a fancy shop front, like a FB Business Page. It serves a purpose for your clients. It can be a credible marker too for PR and media opportunities, but really it isn't the first thing you need to do to build your business.

Glad we resolved that and I hope you agree! I'm not anti-websites; I just see so many women not run with their ideas and inspirations because they don't feel ready. They believe they should have a website first and that just isn't true.

My new website won't be ready until after launching my book, or my new branding, will it stop me -no! Will it matter - no! I have a one-page website that does all I need it to do, ie delivers everything my clients need and sometimes building a business is like building a plane in the sky! JFDI!

When you do build your website, remember:

Your website is not about you, it's a tool to simply deliver what your clients desire.

So write it from your heart space, for your potential, new and existing clients. It must be simple, effective and be underpinned by your brand, key words, and powerful messages. Please don't over complicate it.

How often do you visit other people's websites? Ask why you visit other business leaders' websites? Don't be tempted to hide away your prices or up and coming events. This is often why people visit your website.

Who loves pop ups? Well, there is a reason we have them, but try not to aggravate people off by having a pop up that pops every five seconds. A pop up to see if they want your free e-book, promotion, or newest event is awesome, it could be just what they've visited your site for. Maybe even a low-priced product. Make it nice and easy, and we will talk tech shortly.

Email lists

So many business leaders have no way to connect with their clients in the event FB, or other Social platforms close or crash. Seems unlikely? Well, what control over social media platforms do we actually have? People fail to create their own client list by creating an email list, or they create them and do nothing with them, missing golden opportunities.

Please don't do the above. Growing your client list is crucial to your growth as a business owner. It's protecting your valuable assets and it's creating a link between you and your potential, new, or existing clients, so that if FB crashed today, you could still connect with your clients.

If you haven't got an email list, how long haven't you had one for and how many people might you have potentially missed?

If you do question this, do you have a client email sequence that sends emails to your clients?

If you've grown an email list, do you write frequent emails? If so, how often?

What do you share with your audience? Do you encourage engagement?

How effective are they? Do you measure the open rates and unsubscribes?

I know this can feel frustrating when you have a million other things to work on, and you're probably excited by the prospect of creating a new event, programme or writing a book.

Yet this is really important, and I'd love you to take time to work on this if you haven't already.

There are ways in which to write your email sequence. You don't want to sell, sell, sell.

You should inject your personality into your emails. There are ways to work smarter, building different email sequences for different client entry points. This works really well. Think about if you signed up for a free eBook and received daily emails following for five days, including some free gifts or top tips, got to know your new connection and they invited you to an event? This is a process to help move your clients forwards along their client journey, create connection and trust, and opportunities for you to sell to them.

Your Business Offerings

How you can work smarter is by extending your products and services in the one-to-many way. It doesn't always work for all enterprises, but it does of course work very well for some.

Working intimately, one-to-one, puts a ceiling on your income stream and will limit the number of people you can service in any one time frame. This must feel right for you and you must create a way to ensure your clients always receive the best value from you, whether it's one-to-one or one-to-many. As a business mentor, I know my clients will always get more from working one-to-one with me.

I recognise that no business or business owner is the same and they will all experience different challenges and have different blind spots in their business that if left, can be a catalyst to crisis. If delivering a one-to-many programme, you may not be able to offer that level of care and personal attention; you may not have the opportunity to see that particular blind spot or ask your client intimate questions.

This is why for me, even with my one-to-many models, I will always identify if I need to incorporate some specific time to cover as many different areas or potential blind spots as I can or have online training for the areas some business mentors may not approach, and you may have to consider the same.

I've mentored coaches who have discovered that a more flexible approach works for them. I helped them to align their business to the lifestyle they wanted to design. This is so important for any business owner. You must consider what works for you and ultimately the quality and value you want to deliver to your clients. Along with how your service offerings, business model delivers that.

Tech, Lovely Technology!

Lots of the above requires an element of bringing new technology into your business, maybe design work, new programmes, some of which you may feel confident to do, some will undoubtedly frustrate you, and other tasks you will either not do because you don't enjoy or because you just don't have time.

This is where many business leaders feel the pressure. I do completely understand this. A really good book I can recommend is, 'Who Not How' by Dan Sullivan. This is again another way to work smarter, bring a team together and ensure you're able to work on the areas of your business you enjoy. For many people this is not the tech: hence there are experienced experts out there that can and will do it for you.

I understand the frustrations you may feel, especially in the early stages of your business, when you don't have the resources to invest into outsourcing tech tasks remotely.

I do know the value of doing so, like investing in a business mentor or coach, , when you are scalable and can use available profits to reinvest into growing your business.

Tech in particular is readily available and will not cost you the world, for instance social media automation, streaming services to share live videos over multiple social media platforms or email list management tools. I encourage you to learn how these will work very effectively for you, and how you can implement them into your business to work smarter.

If you're a coach or mentor and building one-to-many online courses, you may wish to consider investing in a learning management tool. I use Karta (other options are available) and this incorporates my email list, payments, landing pages and so much more. A great way to have it all easily available in one space.

All of the above systems and processes are part of your business foundations. Once you're able to begin to recruit talent, you'll feel the release of pressure in many ways, but initially you may not wish to give away control and feel the financial pinch. As you build outwards and scale your business CASH FLOW becomes vital in scaling, investing in teams, software and other means to grow your business. It is important you have a keen eye on cash flow and do not let this get away from you. You must be responsible and know exactly where you are planning ahead for all possibilities or threats to cash flow.

Outsourcing social media content, design work such as branding, landing pages, video content, website building and domain hosting, designing workbooks and course materials to a business operations manager or selection of virtual assistants, to help support you with creation-heavy, time consuming tasks will free you up in so many ways.

However, you must carefully manage your teams and know where you are financially, especially in the early days when growing your business. Learn to let go fast if they are not performing, and give them freedom once you've built trust and results are created regularly. This is a very important aspect of scaling your business. Talent and cash flow become very important, as will your business decisions. Make sure you create solid systems and processes that really support you and your teams to support business growth.

You have and will have worked very hard to get to this point. Be resilient, be aware and make good choices that impact you and your business in a healthy way. I really hope this has helped you - I know each section could have been a chapter.

As I'm writing this book, I'm already seeing how my next one will unfold. There's so much I want to share with you. I do cover all aspects of building Miracle Foundations, systems, and processes that help you to scale up in my The Divine Business Code™ programme. They are so important to your success, wealth and resilience when growing a sustainable, profitable business.

THE POWER OF CONVERSION

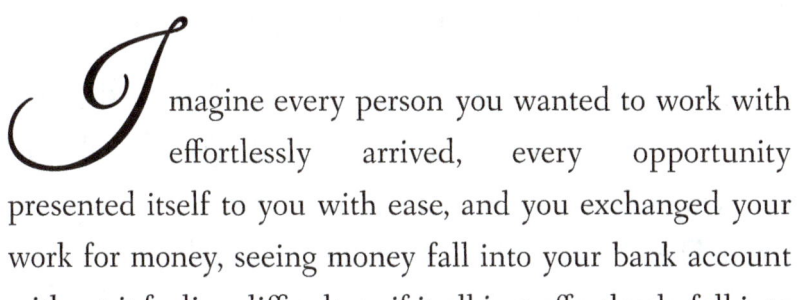

Imagine every person you wanted to work with effortlessly arrived, every opportunity presented itself to you with ease, and you exchanged your work for money, seeing money fall into your bank account without it feeling difficult, as if it all just effortlessly fell into place.

Let me share the real secrets of how to create effortless sales.

To be fair, there are no secrets to sales success. There are ways to work smarter and gain more confidence. There are smarter systems and processes you can integrate into your business. You can begin to make investments of time and money that will maximise opportunities and that will convert to effortless sales, resulting in generating greater profits in your business. Sadly, it's not Magic!

It starts with your mindset, which I'm going to touch on later. It's really important to believe in the products and services you're selling. Instead of selling, imagine them to be really making that difference to your clients and convert sales by confidently selling the many benefits or solutions you bring. Knowing your clients, your products and services, getting really specific, gives you clarity and confidence. Belief will always be your superpower.

The moment you lose belief, you may as well not bother. It's the same when you work a 9-5: if you don't have belief in your employer, you'll walk away or not show up to work as you did before. Belief fuels your passion and desire to create and convert leads with ease.

There are some smarter ways to create a natural increase in leads, which will help you to convert by educating your clients first about you, your credibility, your business, your products and services. We've already covered many in this book, like powerful social media marketing, automated email sequences and of course, having a good coach to help with mindset and confidence, or a business mentor to help with both mindset, confidence and provide you with accountability.

Onboarding Process

Many new business owners miss mapping out an onboarding process. It really is important because it could define why you're so unique and why your clients would choose to buy with you compared to one of your competitors. A client journey makes a difference as to why your clients will come back to you and remain loyal. It's definitely a good place to begin by reminding yourself, visualising how your clients feel when working with you. It will undoubtedly increase the quality of what you already do too.

Think about a client journey. How was it when you followed someone, signed up for their free challenge, then paid to upgrade to their programme, afterwards worked one-to-one with them or went into their membership? It felt natural and you felt special.

The above is not a coincidence. The stepping forward process is mapping out a client journey and onboarding process. It allows you to see the individual experience of each step of your client's journey. You'll be able to refine and review this as you have more clients following each segment of their journey, through feedback and communications.

Consider a shopping experience or online experience. Where you were truly wowed?

What was different? What did you like? What did you not enjoy? Consciously marking these as guiders and reference points to how you design your own client's experiences is really intelligent and will often evoke a deeper connection to wanting to really make sure you look after your clients every step of the way, making sure their experience is the very best you can offer.

This can include taking client information, taking payments easily, claiming upgrades easily, making reordering easy, or even with new clients, sending personalised gifts. These all require systems and processes to ensure they're consistently carried out.

Lead Magnets

One way to help you to grow your audience, and in turn create business opportunities faster and definitely smarter, is to create a lead magnet that says, 'Yes please, I'd like to receive your e-book, full blog or receive the results to my quiz and I'm happy to pass you my email address.' You may have even seen these before. They only work if you incorporate them into your marketing, social media or email marketing, hence the importance of having a structure. I'd suggest not to incorporate them too often and to consider sharing them twice weekly, at opposite sides of the day. What you don't want to do is share them every day and send a vibration that signifies desperation or on the opposite side of the scale forget to shout about your free e-book or low ticket sales products and guess what, no one will sign up or buy them!

Be really creative and tap into what you're guided to do intuitively. Again, experiment and refine, review and most importantly, consider how you can potentially be different. Make your quizzes interactive, your blogs relevant to your audience, and your e-books may work by tagging on a five-day email sequence with more goodies. If you're a therapist or selling products on e-commerce, what can you include that's gifted and builds more trust? i.e., meditations, free samples or readings.

Have a following next step in place, so your audiences aren't just left hanging in the wind, forgetting who you were. You want them to come back keen to learn, enquire, work with you time and again. What you need to be careful to avoid is giving too much away. This could be an opportunity for a low ticket sales that many refer to a trip wire. Such a cold name, but it does allow you to create another incentive for clients to begin to work with you, and it generates a totally passive income.

Gift your whys, and whats away. KEEP your hows for an exchange of gratitude/money.

Lead magnets are also a great way to leave, when leaving a calling card after speaking or being a guest on a podcast show. Rather than, "Visit my website at www... ," instead try, "Come to my website and I have an amazing quiz or eBook all about XXX." It's an incentive for people who have just seen you or listened to you to keep in touch and they already have an inkling if they like what you do, so they're not cold leads, they're warmer. Which leads nicely into podcast shows, and YouTube or FB/Insta TV Shows.

Podcast or TV Shows

Having a podcast show or TV Show is a fantastic way to elevate YOU and your brand and positioning. It gives you access to a far greater audience, creating huge impact and being seen as the 'go to' expert from many parts of the globe. It will require a lot of planning, and like any of the above areas I've touched on, there's a formula for success. However, you can easily start your own show and begin to grow it, or you can go all out and reach out to podcast agencies and invest in having an experienced expert take care of the framework and leg work for you.

Having previously supported Martin, my life partner, in one of his big milestones to creating a podcast show, I have a huge insight into creating a brand-new podcast show, taking it to a TOP TEN UK chart position and successfully running this weekly show for over a full year. Having your own podcast show is invaluable to connecting you more deeply with your potential and existing clients and in a way that accelerates your business growth too. It was a fabulous podcast show, 'Entrepreneur Truths' and now Martin has continued with this show on his own, as it aligns with his brand direction, whilst my efforts are invested in my own brand and business success.

Imagine what a show can do for you in terms of bringing in a new audience and opportunity to showcase who you are and what you do so well. It can be inspiring and deliver a very powerful message. Even being a guest on someone's show will take your name out there to a wider audience. I believe those who need to hear your story will, and the messages you share!

Landing Pages

I love creating lead magnets, trip wires, courses, programmes and getting fiercely creative and using powerful copy and technology to bring them to life, onboarding new clients. What about when you've put together an incredible package and you're now ready to launch your product or service with the world?

Yaaaaayyyy, that feeling of... I'm ready!

Yet are you? Because if you pop a post on social media and expect it to bring in 20/200/2000 clients, let's be honest, is it really going to work? We all know that is highly likely to be a big fat no. You could message your warmer clients you've built a relationship with and sell to them, which is a great way when it is still very early days in business. It also allows you to refine and define your products and services with a smaller audience.

For our Signature programmes, you're really wanting to make that ultimate HUGE impact, so you'll need to consider a smarter way. One which showcases what you're bringing to your client's reach, shares your story, why you know your programme is the best on the market, why you truly believe your potential clients will invest their money in your programme and exactly what they're going to get. The outcomes you may already have, supported by genuine testimonials: there's so much you can incorporate into your landing page.

It's a sales page, ultimately, and I've seen a flood of new entrepreneurs investing their time into building them. Some are incredible, while others are so long I get bored. Like your website, you must remind yourself who they're for and create a client journey, as if you were your customer. Would you read ALL of it? What would you want to read, see, watch on video? The best way to design these is through your clients' eyes; keep them nice and simple. Keep the copy relevant and deliver impact, stand out from everyone else, incorporate your brand and identity, and humour too if you want to. Be BOLD!

ASK FOR THE SALE?

The last but most obvious way to powerfully convert sales is to ASK for the sale. Always use your calls to action in social media posts where needed. Always be honest if you're hosting a challenge or online event that you'll be sharing your latest programme at the start, then see who stays and who's really interested in working with you. Always have open conversations and be intuitively guided when to ask for that sale. This is where you learn to trust in the process and know instinctively when it's the right time to ask.

The people who appreciate and value you will want to work with you. The moment you forget this and go giving, giving, and over giving, you give a piece of you away, for someone who really needs and appreciates it. There is always a fair value of exchange to be had and doing it this way will create a gratitude circle and abundant, confident and positive mindset. If you don't ask, I always say to my clients, how does the universe hear or take your actions seriously? Step up and be heard.

To powerfully convert you must have those conversations and be strong enough to cut out the fluffing around and be direct and ask for the sale. The more you ask, the clearer you are, the more sales you will convert. One thing to remember is sometimes it's a NO, but it may NOT be no forever; it quite often is no, not for now! So, if you receive a no, it's my view to thank them and wish them well with your love and blessings, rather than have a tantrum and be rude or awkward, because they'll never come back to you again. (True colours sometimes show up here too! I've experienced this, and it's very unprofessional. I would not work with someone who made me feel uncomfortable.)

There are many reasons a client can say no. It's not personal, it's often a case of timing or lack of resources. It's ok to ask them for any feedback, but I would not push it. Remember they could come back to you one day, or if you send a poor message, they have the right to share that experience and it will potentially come back to sting you in the backside. Always lead with love and have compassion. Never judge and never convert unethically. What I mean by that is have a standard, a value that supports ethical transactions. If I've ever felt concerned that a client is struggling to pay me, I will clarify that I have always have a scholarship space for each of my programmes, and decline working with them for now, supporting them as much as I can until their circumstances are better and they are in a position to buy my programmes.

LAUNCHING WITH IMPACT

*L*aunching with impact does not just happen.

I want to make this really clear. Having a plan, a proven method, and experience will absolutely help you to reach new levels of success when launching. I'd also like to point out again... the importance of having really grown and nurtured your audience. Being really clear on your powerful marketing messages, and knowing, with not just confidence but real belief, who you are launching to. Get this formula right and you'll begin to see your hard work actually create the levels of impact you desire.

I've tried many launch strategies. If I look back to my first attempts, they were pretty shocking. I would go as far as saying I wasted six months in the online space by knowing what I wanted to sell, having the most incredible courses or mentorship experiences - they still are, so it wasn't about delivering value, or not having a viable product - but what I didn't have was an audience to sell to or an actual plan to launch. I created my packages, promoted them and was so disappointed when I had a small take up. I could have cried. I most probably did. I almost gave up. I'm glad I didn't. I was so frustrated! I was trying to build a perfect product, invested in artwork, copywriters, and tech support without knowing how to launch properly. I don't want you to go through the same.

It's not what you're selling, its who, when and how you're selling

Let me share a way that will not only save you six to twelve months of your time, it will feel a bit weird because you will want to create products and sell, but this is the Golden Ticket to actually seeing your creativity create the levels of impact you desire. It's priceless and I wish I had known this a long time ago... Seriously!

The first piece of advice is to stop working on your final masterpiece, your programme, course or new product. I know that's what many entrepreneurs want to immediately run off and do, but it's not the best way at the beginning. I promise you!

However, if you are at a stage where you've already connected with your audience and have an audience to sell to, by this point you'll be working with paid clients and hopefully be blocking your time out to work on creating your wonderful masterpieces. Yes, please do! But if you have no audience...

You have to focus on building your audience first, being seen and consistently working on this aspect of your business first. This may mean using your personal profile to speak up, creating your own online community, building connections and, firstly and most importantly, trust. Once you've reached that point where you feel you have people following you, working with you and you have client testimonials that you can incorporate into your marketing, then you've reached the next stage of your online business. You must reach this point or it's likely you will fall short on your first launch campaign. We can't just rely on FB advertising campaigns!

Launching five-day online challenges works for many entrepreneurs, but personally I know it's a lot of work. The online world is switching off to it as there are so many challenges out there doing the same thing. You will need to create something different that will appeal to a fresh-eyed audience. They do help build your audience, and they do still work for some business leaders. I also believe you learn a lot about your clients and their learning or buying behaviours and doing challenges does give you a new level of learning experiences that you will take on to support other aspects of your business, like Masterclasses, for example.

Online events are so much fun, but they take a lot of organisation and planning. I love event planning. It's incredible seeing your ideas and inspirations become a reality and again they help to grow and nurture a fresh audience. They also have an incredible impact for those who sign up, delivering exceptional value. The launch of your online or offline event is so hugely important and if you have an audience that's almost waiting for you to launch your next event, it really does make the difference in numbers of sign ups. If you don't have the numbers, there are ways you can accelerate your launch by bringing in affiliates or co-hosting an event with someone who has a wider audience. Of course, paying for FB adverts can also encourage a wider audience, and may be part of your launch strategy, but do not rely on it.

Launches also apply to releasing newly published books, new podcast or TV Shows and this is actually a fantastic place to start and to learn how to successfully plan your launches because oddly, you feel as though you're trying to open the door to a wider audience and indeed, want to reach a wider audience. They're really exciting and because the work you put into creating them is far greater and the investment you will have made is also more significant, you will feel the need to plan deeply, and it encourages a more planned and detailed approach.

All of the above and any launch should be exciting and hold the same degree of planning to ensure it creates a level of excitement and buzz with your audience.

The first thing I do is set a date. How difficult is this?

Open up your calendar and check when you're planning to host your launch day. The ultimate time to allow yourself is twelve to sixteen weeks.

If you're writing a book or launching a podcast, the best way to start this is to begin planning your launch strategy immediately and start by sharing your own journey with your audience, with a provisional date to be publishing or releasing your podcast show. Get them excited and invite your audience to be a part of your journey.

It is important to leave space between your events too, not to overwhelm your audience with too many things for them to sign up to. Give yourself time to pause in between events or they consume you and will leave you feeling mentally and physically exhausted.

The date is set, and you start to share snippets of what you're working on. Invite people to feel excited that something's coming soon and share your excitement and the work you've done to make this possible and maybe some of the challenges too. I believe that sharing real 'in the moment' emotions shows you're human. Think about the people you look up to and how they inspire you: it's by sharing their experiences the highs and the lows, what they thrive in doing and how they overcome them.

Now start by working backwards. Your date for launch; six weeks of marketing your launch, all the organisation or practical tasks you have to do like recording videos, creating workbooks, recording guests for a show, sending T&Cs, all the details including designing the artwork to promote your event, a landing page, updating your website, email sequences to your email list - every single input you need to cover off to create your event.

Working backwards gives you time to cover each aspect of your unique event and plan effectively for its launch. Allow time for delays: you may be ill; something may crop up that affects the design workflow; you may have a new team member that doesn't deliver as expected first time; you may have a tech person who lets you down. This is where talent is an uncontrollable commodity. No one wants anything to go wrong during a launch, but if it happens, by planning for it and giving yourself time to be creative and work through any potential challenges, it allows you to plan much more effectively and won't leave you working till 5am in the morning, burned out and needing two weeks off after your event.

I've created a Launch Successfully PDF for you to download and use as a guide to help you which can be downloaded from my website - www.kellyvikings.com

You may wish to make sure, at least two weeks before your BIG launch, you have all the decks cleared and are fully focused on launching your campaign. It does demand a lot from you if you want to see the results. I've seen many soft touch launches and they're not nearly as effective, yet going all in does demand that extra part of you. I guess it depends on how much you want to see the results at the end.

Here are some insights for you to gain some practical tips to help you with your launch experience. They've all worked for me and after, I'll share what didn't work!

How to plan for your LAUNCH

Event Date (as mentioned)

Event Details and Name

Be creative and ask you audience. Market research is very useful as you can often be too close to your ideas. It gives your audience an opportunity to feel that they're supporting you too.

Target Audience

Really take time to discover who you're creating the event for. Your ideal client. List the features, the benefits, the experiences and testimonials. Anything that creates a connection to deliver your powerful marketing messages.

Marketing for Event - Design Artwork

Prepare for this with ideas and copy, imagery, and any KEY marketing details.

Have templates for promotion with powerful marketing messages, videos and guest interviews. You'll want to initially post six weeks before events, and step this up closer to launch day towards three or four posts a day. Do not make them too salesy, because that turns people off; however, the more awareness you bring to your event, the better. Tag in those who are part of your event and invite them to share to their audience.

Create a landing page with sign up and payment options. Offer an upgrade option if possible. Remember to keep it simple: who it's for and use consistent key words, client centred copy and brand elements along with imagery that matches your promo marketing and event. You will need to upload this onto your website and use an email marketing list or learning management tool to support it and ensure it all connects and is ready before launch day.

Write email templates to go to your email list. Have them ready, with all the copy and links to sign up or join a community, and video links to testimonials. Have this ready to go to your email list and really work hard to make them personal. Don't send twice; don't forget to use their name; don't be afraid to ask them like they're already joining you.

Have a six-week marketing strategy in place and implement it. This is essential, as doing this daily will prove challenging. Have it all ready, using the formulas I provided earlier and making sure that where needed you have calls to action. Know how you'll be communicating your launch and have all the copy written in advance, saved onto a Word doc. If you have an auto scheduler, schedule it. Keep it on point and let people know if you're doing lives in advance. If you're emailing your email list, keep this consistent to the copy you're sharing so it sends out a strong marketing messages both online and offline.

Prepare testimonials as social proof. Use these in your marketing campaigns. If you've hosted an event before or recorded your guests for a podcast, ask for feedback and share it. Then it's not just you sharing proof of what you've created or what it will do for your audience. It's very powerful to share testimonials.

Plan for an event FB Group to be set up, if required, and set up all group rules, schedule events and get ready to welcome your audience, including a welcome video. Get this set up with matching imagery already to go. Make someone else an admin as well. You'll need to do this to safeguard you in the event that FB bans you at all during promotion, for any perceived over-promotion. I've seen this happen a lot and it just keeps you available to hop in if there's any external challenges.

Ask your existing clients if they'd enjoy helping you promote your event. A bit obvious, but another way to expand outside your available audience and it brings them into your journey with you. Plus, it actually elevates your energy, knowing you have loyal supporters.

Interview your event guests on social media prior to your event. Bringing in your guests and interviewing them before your event creates an opportunity for promotion and for your potential clients to get a feel for who they're signing up to see across all social media platforms.

I love this, because it creates a real synergy and gets you seen; it creates real impact before your event.

Set up a WhatsApp or external group away from social media to encourage you, especially for a podcast or book promo. THIS is what helped my partner and me reach No. 8 in the UK charts for our podcast show. An offline WhatsApp group gave clear directions on how our support group could help us. Again, this takes some planning. You can have all the messages readily available on a Word doc and set to go with links to destinations, posts, iTunes episodes, etc.

Plan how you can share your launch and details with a wider audience through guest speaking opportunities available online or media/PR/Radio opportunities. Get out there and share what you're doing; get it out to as many public places you can be seen. Tap into your guests' audiences or connections' audiences, even their podcast shows. This is a great way for you to be seen and create even more impact for your BIG launch.

As you're promoting, ask your connections to share and invite anyone they know who would love to join you. If you don't ask your clients, friends or family, or anyone who genuinely supports you, how can you naturally assume they'll know to support you? It never hurts to ask.

Plan for a BONUS sign up now! A final big reveal to really encourage those sat on the fence. This is great to do the weekend before you open the doors to your event, with last-minute sign up opportunities. Bring a fantastic opportunity, a BONUS to your event. Of course, this will be extended to all those who sign up, but it does incentivise anyone who is almost wanting to sign up to actually do it!

As you can see, there's much more to do than just create an event, pop out a few posts and just hope people sign up. That doesn't happen, just like being an overnight success doesn't, and the more you try these things the more you'll see what's working for you and your audience and what's bringing you the most success and results.

I've launched an online event four weeks before the launch date. It had over twenty speakers and ran for two weeks. It was a great success and I loved every minute, so it can be done in many ways, but I know I'll have missed many other opportunities and I was so exhausted by the end of it, I literally needed an entire week off to recover. This is not advisable or productive for you or your existing clients and 'I knew' what I was doing, having organised, managed and run over a hundred events in my full business career.

What doesn't work is failing to prepare and not planning. Failing to be unique and not testing your ideal client market. Not adapting your launch to the current circumstances externally going on in the world. Not being flexible and allowing that space in between. What also doesn't work is not communicating the actual benefits of your events. Features are not what sell your product or service, it's the experiences your client takes away and the benefits they gain from attending.

Do map out your launch strategy using the valuable information above. When you have successfully launched your first event, programme, book, or podcast, take time to breathe. Enjoy that power of pause. Creating, planning, launching and running events is mentally consuming. Take that time to recharge and reflect.

In these moments after a big launch, I recommend to my clients that they REFINE every aspect of their launch. What went well and what didn't and how can they improve and what do they remove next time? The learning through application can always be improved upon and when you reach a particular level in launching, you can up level your affiliate programmes and really learn how to create an even bigger impact.

Good luck with your launches. I know how hard you'll have worked to create these moments. I hope what I've shared really helps and you do learn to start from the beginning.

I've had to step backwards to really grow my audience and define and position myself and there's no shame in doing this either. The real growth comes in the pauses, or gaps.

Let me know when you're launching and celebrating your new successes. I want to hear all about it! I am also happy to support or help if I can in any way.

THE POWER OF PAUSE

Building the business of your dreams is truly amazing. It must begin somewhere, and yet it never really feels like it ends. As women business leaders we often work so hard, push ourselves to the point we are so tired, that we forget to listen to what our bodies naturally need. We fail to honour ourselves and put ourselves first which often leads to overwhelm, burn out or generally feeling so friggin' tired it's extremely difficult to enjoy harmony and balance in our life. Why do we find it so hard to surrender?

Your business needs <u>you</u> to grow it, but your life demands that <u>you</u> take 'The Power of Pause' to fulfil your divine destiny and ultimate life path. For us to really recognise the moments to pause, we must connect within our heart space, self-knowing, honouring and this can often feel selfish.

Well, this is your permission ladies, because listen up, the more you avoid it the harder it is to truly shine. The glow that emanates from your soul will glow brighter, allowing you to stop and enjoy the rewards of pausing, being truly present. That glow attracts everything you desire effortlessly; it creates harmony and flow in your life; it's like a secret magnet that attracts with ease. Make time for it. It is not selfish, it is self-love and compassion for who you are, all you do, and what you stand for in this world.

For no woman in our world, no matter where she is, or her age, colour or size none of this should matter. EVERY woman in the world deserves the opportunity to shine and set herself free, stepping forwards into her Divine Ultimate Power.

I believe in the magnificence of every woman, and this is why I'm so passionate about supporting women in business to really thrive, to show up unapologetically as themselves, and to never turn back; to step forwards into their ultimate divine energy, their power and own that shit! To be proud of who they are! Unity, Equality and Inclusion are integral to our New World and gifting every woman her voice and Divine Power.

The world is big enough for everyone to succeed and the more women in business I can help the better. Hence I wrote this book for you and all Divine Business Warriors. I committed to it, I invested in it and I have contributed to writing daily for over two months, putting my work on pause to bring this to you through my greatest mission to inspire love, a deeper connection and help activate the following truth:

> "Every woman deserves to shine her unique divine feminine power to the world"
>
> — KELLY VIKINGS

So how do we, amongst a million other things, take that time for us. Trust me, you are talking to a lady who was so in the middle of a shit storm for several years, decades, that not only did I hide behind a mask, I also never stopped. What was I running from, what was I hiding and who put that pressure on me? Maybe you need to ask the same questions?

Am I hiding the real me behind a mask?

Do I ever stop and take time for me?

What do I run from?

What or who am I hiding from?

Who puts the pressure on me?

I can guess what your replies will be, but I will let you discover them for yourselves. You see, you may notice the answers need addressing; you know the truths. Only when you take them away and actually do something with them will you consider stopping and actually doing something with the answers, there is always something you can find to distract you from addressing your truths.

But what if The Universe says, Hey... Listen, precious lady. If you don't stop to listen and slow down, stop living a life where your internal world does not mirror your outside, external world, it will FORCE you to stop. So, you really have a choice, and guess what? When you truly do stop and take time to honour your soul and life with balance and harmony, it is exactly at that point you are able to step into your power and in the moments of calm and space you realise the magic appears effortlessly.

If something from your past holds you back, this is where my free 30 day programme comes into its own because stepping into your power, Divine Alignment allows you to let go of those shadows. Pain can hurt, and failures and setbacks hurt too, but healing through these moments in our life frees us and we don't have to live a life sentence. We can heal and learn, grow forwards. Nothing, even our deepest fears or subconscious doubts, nothing should stand in our way.

When we free ourselves from this darkness, we step forwards onto our authentic life path towards spiritual fulfilment and the more you recognise what you were born to become. We are not only fulfilled, we become spiritually aligned, and this is also where I have found that real strength, energy and strength, success and wealth shine.

How is your relationship with yourself? Take time to get to know you. Connect with your divine self and understanding who she is. Self-love and compassion are learning to trust in yourself too. Listen to those moments when you require to take time for you and live-in natural flow. Love in action is a real embodiment of self-love.

Practise taking time for gratitude and even honour your future self with daily rituals such as visualisation, meditation, breath work, exercise and grounding. Protect your energy, environment and sacred space. Celebrate who you are, the wins you have daily; however small or big they are, they are yours.

I've worked with five of the enlightened mothers in my work with Divine Feminine. Stepping into your authenticity, and power with grace takes many commitments. To truly claim your power, your voice you must learn to embrace the power of pause and listen to your soul.

Yet to really connect with your truth, it takes an awareness of listening to your truth. This is discovering your innate knowing. This is where viewing from your heart space becomes very powerful and if you listen, you can really begin to trust in that connection between yourself and your energy space. This allows you to truly shine as the real you and protect her from the pulls of the external world, creating a stronger, more powerful forward, natural, harmonious state of flow. Divine Alignment™ creates a world where both your internal and external worlds glide effortlessly and in unity. This creates space for a limitless, balanced and harmonious life.

It is what I choose now. many ways I celebrate this is my working week, when I take time for me and how I choose to live daily, my nutritional choices and spiritual choices. I don't always get this perfect. I do have to work hard to maintain this balance and harmony because I know it isn't natural for me, yet it powerfully supports me to be the truest, highest version of myself. I honour this daily. When I make mistakes, I look for the lessons not the punishment.

I was looking for external gratitude, material success, to feel wanted by a business community, due to childhood vulnerabilities and multiple setbacks. I was putting that pressure on myself and wearing a mask. No one else was forcing me to work eighty-hour weeks.

This is why I share this with you also because if you want to find the answers, they're already inside you. Knowing them requires continuous work and sometimes you may falter. That's ok too because we all do. Let's all learn and move forwards, creating a better way for everyone. I want you to embody who you are, take that time to create space for you, preserve your energy on what truly matters and honour yourselves by making the best choices. I would love for you to practise this daily and to pass it on to many others because we can all contribute to creating the change we wish to see in our worlds.

What we do has a ripple of impact. It creates waves and by creating waves we change lives, one at a time. What ripple do you want to leave for future generations? To work so hard they break? To accrue debts and stretch themselves financially and to make mistakes and suffer for a lifetime? Or to live a life of purpose, a divine sense of self fulfilment and appreciation of what really matters to them and future generations where they leave a footprint of hope, faith and unity living their fullest expressions?

In your lifetime and for future generations let's welcome new cycles, leading with love and working together to create unity, harmony and balance so that as women we don't forget ourselves, we don't break ourselves, we step into our truest highest power, and we shine a beacon to so many others.

I want you to believe this is possible, for you to know it is possible and to step out from any shadow to reveal your truest, highest self. Claim her back: she is within you; she wants to shine brightly. The question is, do you want to? Are you ready to step into your power?

RESILIENCE AND GROWTH

During the two years I was rediscovering myself and healing from a lifetime of pain, setbacks and failures, one of the most significant things for me was actually sharing my truths. I did so by sharing my story of business failure, and the emotions I was experiencing like deep grief of loss, shame, guilt, and how I was so full of anxiety, and how I was so very close to taking my own life.

You see, all my life I've had to respond to crisis, the uncontrollable and extreme vulnerabilities. I've had to tap into unwavering amounts of intuition and my resilience muscle has been used more than most people's, which is why every time, I was able to pick up and move forwards. It became easier to do so. It's a muscle we all have within us; our innate strength and resilience is truly remarkable at times.

My story is a little extreme, yet I've known many more people survive the most unfortunate of events and how they move forward, and then inspire others, is just remarkable.

During the last two years, at various times, to get constructive feedback, I've asked my audience to describe me, with words, in order to identify myself in business, to encapsulate 'a fame name'. For instance…I am the 'XXX'. What came back was firstly – Resilient, and secondly – Growth Leader so I began to use The Resilience and Growth Leader. It felt so right, and I wanted at the time to break down barriers of failure with my truths and inspire other women to realise that any setback was in fact a gift, to move forwards with Strength, Resilience and Survival Wings.

It's something I'm still incredibly passionate about, although my own brand identity has evolved and so has my business model. I still carry the same mission to empower and protect women in business. This is why talking about Resilience and Growth is so important to me. I talk openly and honestly about my own experiences; I show people that taking responsibility for what happened is crucial for their growth. It also helps others to understand that unless you were in that arena, that you were the one with the sweat and blood on your face, getting knocked down, you do not know and would never know the circumstances and cannot and should never judge. I also show that the scars you have on your back are reminders, markers of how far you've moved forwards, and that the greatest lessons we learn are in those moments. Taking all of the lessons I've learnt in those moments, I share them to protect other women in business and this for me is so important!

Resilience is about having a wider perspective, how you navigated crisis before, in, and after any given circumstance. It's about how you bounce back, or forwards as I say, and what you do with the lessons you learnt in those moments. It would have been so easy for me to not try to save my business. I didn't. I committed to trying to save it and did the best I could in every moment of failure. It would've been easy, after all of it, for me to take my life. To disappear. Yet something kept me here.

I knew I had to share the real truths, to stand in my truths for others to see and learn from. It would've been easy to hide away. I could've not tried again and disappeared. Many of my family judged me; they definitely didn't support me. Those I had helped and genuinely given to through my business disappeared; they didn't support me. I could have easily given up, but something shook me and was a strong catalyst to trying again, doing what I love and discovering a new way forward. This is resilience and growth.

How can we all become more resilient? How can we all encourage growth not just in business but in ourselves and our businesses? Having a transparency of where you are, and what potential threats there are, is crucial. Making logical and heart led, intuitive decisions is absolutely necessary. Yes, you can use all three of these to navigate your internal and external words. Set intentions and goals, but don't just set them, measure them, prioritise them and hold yourself accountable, responsible for them.

Learn and review your strengths and weaknesses, either with you or your external factors, with influences in your immediate life, and with your teams. Use reviewing and refining processes like the ones we've covered in this book. Don't just allow your business to overtake you, but actually drive your business and make it work for you. Have a healthy and encouraging view of your cash flow and know exactly where you're able to make logical decisions on your investments into scaling your business or investing in your own personal development.

When we're faced with external pressures, it's easy to create an overwhelm cycle. We avoid, we 'hope' things will get better, we create an imaginable outcome that 'things may or will work out' and being resilient is not easy at times. However, it's so important to ask and question the elephant in the room... What if they don't work out? What if you don't do 'X'? What if you don't make 'X' this month? Planning and projecting in business is crucial for gaining clarity, learning specificity and managing your expectations and that for others.

I would always have a ninety-day business plan and work with it. Keeping your eyes on longer and shorter term goals too. Not only can you see where your weaknesses are, but you can observe patterns and work ahead for any potential threat. So many business owners fail to STOP because they're so engrained in their business and burn themselves out in the process for too long. Often small tweaks to a business can have a huge impact and divert pressure and create smarter pathways to success. You can do this yourself by writing your own ninety-day plan.

I identify these when I work with my clients, by observation of blind spots and a logical outside perspective of their business. It's a very healthy approach to take. Many people say I'm so lovely: heart led and passionate I am, but equally, I can be a real kick ass mentor, because I KNOW what happens if the shit hits the fan on a huge scale and the possible outcomes if that happens. I'm not scared to ask the many questions often avoided by other mentors.

Bringing everything together in this book creates a quantum leap of truly aligned success and that's what I want for every reader. I wanted to gift you as much as I possibly could and also for you to recognise what works, but equally, to have your eyes wide open to what if it doesn't!

Aside from setting constant markers for growth in your business and reviewing them frequently, and consciously making business decisions that support better outcomes in your business, what else can you do? You must have an eager, reactive eye on the two biggest areas of focus in your business, those being... cash flow and talent, i.e., teams. This includes your health and mindset too! I make it very clear that when you're always working in the midst of your business, you must also be able to step out and see exactly where you are in terms of your cash flow and talent. This is absolutely crucial for navigating your business, but also helps any quick decisions that need to be made. Too many business owners don't factor their cash flow into their business plan. Where they are today, right now! What they're even working towards, the future! It's crazy: you may as well set off on an ultra-marathon without any experience and just wing it.

You must learn, from the very start of your business, how to navigate cash flow and make it work smarter for you. Scaling up is one thing but scaling down is quite another.

Scaling down does not mean closure, it means making cutbacks now for, and maybe a brighter future that you could have completely missed if you hadn't planned for it. Scaling up brings another dynamic, of course, because you will want to identify what investments you make and you can only do this with conscious intent if you have a real insight, depth of knowledge and certainty of exactly where your business is and a measure of how you got to where you are.

It's a constant strategy: plan, action, refine, review and implement process which, if mastered, is like a beautiful, magical, purpose driven masterpiece.

KNOW YOUR

BUSINESS

NUMBERS

TALENT

CASH

ACT fast

Make smart decisions based on historical evidence and current positioning. It's your business. No one can make those decisions but you. Be aware of the risks if you don't act quick enough. Are you making decisions under immense pressure or are you making decision whilst you're sucked in too deep working in your business? Resilience will teach you how to make decisions in the calm and be prepared for what comes at you, allowing you to respond quickly and much more effectively.

CREATING YOUR LEGACY

I almost feel sad, writing my final chapter. It really has been an honour to share as much as I have with you over these chapters. Thank you for reading them, let me know if you've enjoyed them, if I've helped you in any way or you wish to stay in touch. I'm not just an author that disappears, I value connection over anything, so please do connect with me.

Creating our legacy embodies so much of what I've shared throughout the book. I know your business means so much more to you than it just being a business. I want to share some important and powerful messages with you. Each one of them supports you in equal measures to create your legacy that isn't just your business but has supported you to step into your full power, has supported your family and your aspirations for life, and has given you a real divine purpose that leaves a lasting legacy.

Remember, we never know how many lives we truly impact. We must be responsible, heart and purpose led leaders, standing tall in our truth, leading with love and a little spark of Viking Warrior spirit. Be the example of the standards you wish to lead by, always leading with LOVE!

Self-Love - It will always start with you.

Everything does. Connection to yourself first is so, so important. I really would love for you to have learnt, honoured and celebrated this. Just ten minutes in the morning, when you feel you need to, and make the weekends or two days a week about doing what serves you. There is so much more to life than admin and paperwork, and you will enjoy your life and look back, knowing you've created a lasting legacy that's shown it's possible and you've led the way for so many other women to love themselves first. That's compassion at its finest.

The past is not the measure of your future.

Please do not sit in the past. Old beliefs, habits or other people's old judgements do not serve you today, now in this moment or your future self. Bitter people sit in their past; unhappy people cast aspersions; jealous people judge. You owe it to yourself to take responsibility for you. No one else will or can. If you're unhappy, want better, judge other people, or bitch and moan, now is the time to STOP! Free yourself from all that B.S. and take a good hard look in the mirror. As harsh as this seems, if you see yourself and know you turn up, show up and are always your best self, and you remove the limitations or expectations of others and rely solely on yourself, then you're looking at the real truth. The real you and you're ready to set free and step forwards to create your legacy, to live your Life Path.

Free and limitless

We were all born into this world to live a human existence, bringing with us lessons we needed to be taught. We all have a unique DNA and whatever it is we're here to do, understanding yourself and embodying that wisdom will ultimately set you on a path to freedom. The limits we set upon ourselves are equally our choice as to whether we live by them or not. We all have an innate purpose, a calling. If we know who we are and trust in this, we not only set ourselves free, but step into a life of limitless possibilities.

Not the equation of anyone else

No one else has your DNA, your past life experiences in this world or any other lifetime. Judgement of ourselves is cast by our expectations and only we know the truth of our past, present and future. You decide what legacy you wish to create and don't judge its size by anyone else's perspective or historical reference. This is your legacy, no one else's. I see too many women playing safe, not through choice, but comfort, scared to see what lies on the other side of hiding in the shadows or allowing fear to limit their full potential. What will people think? What happens if I don't achieve it? Too scared to want to make their first million pounds. Why not? If it fuels your future aspirations and carves your Divine Purpose in life, f*%k everyone else. You dream as big as you friggin' well desire!

Build life on your terms - An exceptional life does not just happen.

Just ensure you don't get caught in a hustle, grind, pointless lifestyle, where you forget what meaning is, or forget for what purpose you started this mission. I always have a vision board, and I work towards my highest goals and share gratitude daily for stepping closer towards them. Don't forget what it is you're building and the reasons why. If you want a freer life, or travel, or financial security, work towards this and make it happen. Work towards those goals and visualise them every day.

Get out of your head into your heart space

It can all get a bit crazy at times, I know this. As women we are 'master juggler machines' but remember to take that important time to get out of your own head. Otherwise, you won't think clearly, and you'll disconnect. The body knows you; it will remind you. It's so important to get out of your head and into your heart space: ground, breathe, meditate, dance, go swimming in the ocean, walk under the moonlight, pick your flowers from the garden, connect to it. You'll feel so much more grounded, connected and your work will flow. Your health and energy will thank you too. Or, if you're like me you'll be as woo woo as you can and conjure your wiccan magick, get grounding in the forest and really deeply connect to mother nature.

Learn to honour your energy and fill your cup first

I'm not going to preach what I've not had to learn. This for me has been my hardest lesson to learn. HONOUR your energy first! It's so easy to say yes, to just message that one person, to do that Zoom when you've been on the go all day and you're really tired, to cook that big family meal when you've worked hard all week and are very exhausted. To not exercise because you're writing your book in the mornings and are too tired as the day goes on... Oops, mini confession!

(I did walk daily, I promise.) Fill your own cup first. Again, like I've mentioned, you will feel so much more grounded, connected and your work will flow. Your health and energy will thank you too. You will have more to serve from and give.

Be clear on your WHY

Don't forget your WHY. If it all becomes too much, or you reach a point where you get bored or growing your business and creating your legacy does not serve you, make decisions that do serve you and your destiny. We all evolve, things do change, you may want to walk away and sell your empire. You may be at a stage where you're ready to create a new divine path. As long as you're stepping forwards purposefully and it serves your soul, that's what's important. Remember your WHY!

Be prepared to face setbacks - Success will TEST YOU

I really wish I could guarantee a business that if you follow this book and do everything I've shared, your business will grow, and success, wealth and prosperity are all coming your way. It's going to be so friggin' easy and you'll LOVE every single day. I wish I could wave a magic wand. Sadly, I can't and to be honest, those knocks and setbacks are tests of strength, resilience and character. They're what shape you.

We'll all be tested in our path towards success. The more we look to learn, enquire, grow through them and because of them, the brighter our future becomes and the more the universe sees our truth and intent.

Be clear on your MISSION - have a North Star and be focused inside your lane

Your Business is not the same as anyone else's. It does NOT fit inside a one size fits all box. This is why having that resilient plan and knowing where you are, growing forwards and sometimes taking stepping back, allows you to navigate towards your North Star. Your route will be different, how long it takes you will be different, you may have to jump more loops, or navigate more shit storms, but the clearer you are... the more focused you are... the faster you will grow and scale your business by taking aligned, inspired action.

Changing LIVES starts with One Person, One Vision, One Action

I know how easy it is to think our biggest aspirations are just unreachable. How can I possibly achieve this? It's so easy to get caught up in the bigger picture and place those expectations on yourself. What I suggest is to have that legacy, the one you want to create. Start by working towards it, without any expectations, just desires, and one step at a time, one vision, think of the one life, then the collective lives that you can change. It just takes that one spark of inspiration that can be enough to set you on the path towards fulfilment. The right people will present themselves to you, serving you with new lessons, new opportunities one person at a time. It's having the confidence and BELIEF to just make a start!

Make a contribution

I couldn't write about creating a legacy without a powerful message about one of my personally favourite things. Making a contribution! To yourself, others, communities, society, a lasting legacy that creates a wave of impact like an online FB community I initiated.

Divine Feminine - Women in Business

It was not about me, and it isn't today, it's about something far bigger! I invited 11 other community leaders to step up and contribute to creating this incredible, powerful community where we all contribute to empowering other women in business.

It is a community where every woman is equal. We celebrate supporting each other and our unique gifts and are making a real difference to women's lives from all over the world. This is about stepping into our power, embodying balance and harmony and spirituality, honouring ourselves, each other and awakening Divine Feminine Energy.

Embody leading with LOVE

Which leads me beautifully to Leading with LOVE, which is something I've naturally done since I was tiny, lighting up the room, my office, communities, and all those special to me. I learnt how to intuitively move forwards, accepting and forgiving, and it wasn't until I worked with The Divine Feminine, our five enlightened mothers, Kuan Yin, Isis, Mother Mary, Tara & Kali , that I recognised the true magnificence of this and how this could be integrated into every woman's heart space and be so powerfully for themselves and for humankind. Leading with love is a beautiful place to be. Embodying this is completely freeing and is without a doubt a beautiful beacon of LOVE to shine to others, every single day.

Creating your Legacy

There is nothing more rewarding than seeing your aspirations, inspirations, intentions, dreams, whatever you wish to call them, come into the world and create their ripples of impact on whatever scale your legacy had intended. I want you to reach for your dreams and recognise the incredible work you're doing. As entrepreneurs that energy is magical. I love seeing the effects that magic inspires within people.

It's incredible. You enjoy every moment and make sure you know when you've achieved each step towards creating your longer-term legacy. YOU ARE A LEGACY CREATOR.

Celebrate your wins

When you are so intensely, passionately and deeply driven to work towards your legacies, you must celebrate the wins, your incredible achievements every step of the way. The importance of this is huge, especially as women, because of the pressure that we sometimes put on ourselves. It clouds the present moments and space in which we can hold ourselves high and know we've done something very special. We all deserve moments like this. You take that precious time to celebrate. A little tip here is to have a weekly agenda, make it happen and celebrate your wins. Take weekly steps that activate your Divine Business Success Code.

Remember nothing can hold you back; you are free; you are limitless

I'm hoping that by reading The Divine Business Code you will not only recognise how far you've come, but also what's possible. I've given you my advice based on my experiences; I know my advice works, because I've worked with many clients who are seeing the results work for them too. One thing we must always remember to do is to STEP UP, not let anything or anyone stand in our way, least of all ourselves.

> "YOU ARE DESTINED FOR EVEN GREATER SUCCESS"

Are you ready to step into your Ultimate Power?

To manifest your unique Divine Alignment;

to realise greater strength, wealth & financial prosperity;

by activating the sacred knowledge of The Divine Business Code!

> "YOU ARE LIMITLESS"

I know because if I can overcome what I have and keep stepping forwards, creating my own level of quantum success, leading with LOVE and creating my supreme legacy, my calling in life, supporting women just like you Divine Feminine - Women in Business... you can too!

www.ingramcontent.com/pod-product-compliance
Lightning Source LLC
Chambersburg PA
CBHW070040230426
43661CB00034B/1439/J